SIMPLICITY WINS

SIMPLICITY WINS
How Germany's Mid-Sized
Industrial Companies Succeed

✦ ✦ ✦ ✦ ✦ ✦ ✦ ✦ ✦ ✦ ✦ ✦

Günter Rommel ✦ Jürgen Kluge
Rolf-Dieter Kempis
Raimund Diederichs ✦ Felix Brück
McKinsey & Company, Inc.

HARVARD BUSINESS SCHOOL PRESS
BOSTON, MASSACHUSETTS

Copyright © 1995 by McKinsey & Company, Inc.
This edition published by arrangement with
Schäffer-Poeschel Verlag, Stuttgart
First published as *Einfach überlegen:
das Unternehmenskonzept, das die Schlanken schlank
und die Schnellen schnell macht*
All rights reserved
Printed in the United States of America
99 98 97 96 95   5 4 3 2 1

Library of Congress Cataloging-in-Publication Data

Einfach überlegen. English.
    Simplicity wins : how Germany's mid-sized industrial
companies succeed / Günter Rommel . . . [et al.].
        p.   cm.
    Includes index.
    ISBN 0-87584-504-5
    1. Small business—Germany—Management.
2. Management—Germany.   3. Organizational effectiveness—Germany.   I. Rommel, Günter.   II. Title.
HD62.7.E3913   1995   94-34599
658.02'2'0943—dc20   CIP

The paper used in this publication meets the requirements
of the American National Standard for Permanence of
Paper for Printed Library Materials Z39.49-1984.

CONTENTS

✦ ✦ ✦ ✦ ✦ ✦ ✦ ✦ ✦ ✦ ✦ ✦

FOREWORD

✦ ✦ ✦ ✦ ✦ ✦ ✦ ✦ ✦ ✦ ✦ ✦

*B*RILLIANT ideas and solutions in any field often possess a blinding simplicity. Engineering and science are no exception, with their constant endeavors to arrive at simple solutions from complex, unwieldy constructs—for example, replacing complicated multistage syntheses with single-stage direct syntheses in the production of acrylic fiber. In economics, too, it was no coincidence that the simple exchange mechanism of money took the place of laborious bartering. And as a final example, pension insurance could perhaps be interpreted as a simplification of the principle of philoprogenitiveness as a means of providing for old age.

As my colleagues demonstrate here, companies often stray in the opposite direction. Simple product ranges, organization structures, and procedures slowly but surely attract increasing deposits of parts and variants, layers and branches, with the result that escalating variety and extreme self-sufficiency in the value-added chain cripple mobility—and competitiveness.

To my knowledge, this book is the first time that the inference has been conclusively elaborated on such a sound quantitative basis. It will inevitably open up startling new horizons. It will certainly capture the attention of decision makers aware of the temptation to respond to increasingly complicated external demands with matching internal complexity. Of the few machinery and component manufacturers with truly excellent performance in profitability and growth, every single one is more simply organized throughout than those with less outstanding performance. Moreover, the differences in performance can generally be explained by simplicity alone.

This insight into what made outstanding companies so successful was also confirmation of McKinsey findings that came, as it were, from the opposite direction: from pursuing the issue of why some companies performed so much worse than others in comparable situations. The key weaknesses turned out to be overbroad product offerings, overlong value-added chains, and overcentralized business functions—in other words, overcomplexity. Furthermore, our projects in this area revealed that radical complexity reduction normally improved returns so much that the companies involved could draw level with, or even overtake, their most profitable competitors.

The two different approaches—identifying the common characteristics of successful companies to explain outstanding performance on the one hand, and searching for tangible sources of below-average performance on the other—were pursued independently. The fact that the results agree so well gives us grounds for optimism. Having been, so to speak, checked and double-checked, such findings should mobilize the entrepreneurial energy to develop enormous, unexploited profit potentials. All the more so, since the practice of the successful "simple" companies and experience with radical complexity reduction give concrete pointers as to how to make the change and how to turn potential into business reality.

The "simplicity wins" formula in no way contradicts the many management concepts that expound the sources of corporate excellence—for example, lean production or time-based management.

The effects of simplicity, as portrayed here, go far below the symptomatic level. Many of the basics identified in earlier analyses of success at excellent companies can either be traced directly to simplicity—or low complexity—or are a prerequisite for it. Simplicity is the principle that makes the lean, lean and the mean, mean.

This simplicity will become a new force in the competitive struggle. The aim of this book is to provide inspiration for such a change in management culture in the 1990s.

— Dr. Michael Roever
Director
Munich Office
McKinsey & Company, Inc.

PREFACE

✦ ✦ ✦ ✦ ✦ ✦ ✦ ✦ ✦ ✦ ✦ ✦

$\mathcal{F}$ROM 1985 to 1989, the growth rate of some mid-sized German machinery and component manufacturing companies was outstanding—more than twice that of their competitors. What was behind this phenomenal growth? Why were some of these companies—in particular, machine-tool and textile machinery builders, component suppliers, and white goods makers—superior in all three dimensions of operating efficiency: cost, time, and quality?

To try to find the answers, McKinsey & Company's German offices conducted the German "simplicity" survey, so called because one clear message that emerged was that simplicity—in a company's product range, customer base, organization structure, and business system—is key to corporate success.

The intellectual inspiration for the inquiry dates back to 1988, when McKinsey consultants who work in the area of operations held a conference in Puerto Rico. While the materials presented at the conference formed a well-integrated overall operations concept and provided a strong intellectual base to inform work with clients on operations issues, participants felt that the analysis and approaches presented would be considerably enhanced if the existing concept were developed further and supported by an international database on performance dimensions.

Accordingly, they agreed on several objectives for an industry-wide survey: identify industry-specific success factors; classify success patterns by weighting individual factors and clarifying their interrelationships; develop a cohesive concept for manufacturing strategy; demonstrate the significance of operations strategy in overall company success; and establish a database. Toward the end of 1989, the participating McKinsey partners decided to go ahead with the manufacturing competitiveness survey under the leadership of Günter Rommel, then a director in the firm's Stuttgart office and now managing director of the firm's office in Tokyo.

The entire Puerto Rico conference group spent several weeks preparing the questionnaire, which was further modified after dry runs with two companies. The Technical University in Darmstadt, which had cooperated in a 1984–1985 survey that looked at the use of computer technologies in the German machinery industry, was approached again and agreed to participate in the project by helping to develop the questionnaire, conducting some of the interviews, and performing some of the quantitative analysis.

The university team—a professor, two Ph.D. students, and a number of master's students—collaborated with the McKinsey team from the early stages so that all survey team members were in agreement as to what they were looking for. The preparation and development of the questionnaire was a collaborative effort, bringing together McKinsey's consulting experience and knowledge of the sectors involved and the university's research capability.

Once the questionnaire and other preparations were complete, the team approached a long list of companies that they had selected for study. These companies had been selected on the basis of their performance records between 1985 and 1989 in growth, return on sales, and liquidity. The CEOs of the companies approached were promised, in return for their participation, a report positioning their company against the cross-industry benchmarks that would be identified.

A total of 40 companies chose to participate. The survey took the form of a questionnaire to discover approaches and data and a number of interviews at all levels within each company. First, a company's CEO was interviewed for two to three hours by a senior McKinsey consultant and one or two students. Following the interview, the students worked with the functional heads at the company to fill out the 164-item questionnaire.

Further interviews were held as necessary to clarify and interpret these data. When all the interviews and data collection had been completed, two McKinsey consultants worked with the Darmstadt students to develop a first cut of the results, which were then presented to the survey team in a two-day workshop.

Over 2,000 items of data per company were assembled to provide a comprehensive picture of the success patterns among competitors in the German machinery and components manufacturing industries. Detailed and intensive analysis revealed patterns that clearly separated the most successful companies from the least successful in the survey sample. In most cases, the differences were significant: there was a strong correlation between the practice of "simplicity" and corporate success. Thirty-nine of the 40 companies were clustered into 13-company groups of the best, good, and least-successful competitors; data on one participating company were insufficient.

At the end of 1990 and in early 1991, about a year after the survey was initially planned, the team began rolling out the results. Since the survey in Germany, McKinsey has completed a project that broadens the survey's scope to include a sample of companies in the United States.

October 1994

ACKNOWLEDGMENTS

This book is a team effort, and not just because it has five authors. The underlying data and analyses are the result of intensive collaboration with mid-sized machinery and component manufacturing companies, which confirmed the importance of simplicity as a winning factor in business. The project also benefited from the cooperation of numerous colleagues in McKinsey's offices around the world, and especially in Germany and Cleveland, many of whom made important contributions to the analysis and presentation of the contents. And our colleague Steve Walleck, formerly a director in McKinsey's Cleveland office, also lent the project his enthusiastic support and wrote the Postscript to this English-language edition.

Above all, we would like to thank the many top managers who acted as their companies' spokespeople in the course of the survey. We also owe a debt of gratitude to the Technical University in Darmstadt; without the contribution of Professor Herbert Schulz and the untiring commitment of his project manager, Ralph Wiegland, the resulting comprehensive database would never have been built. And our special thanks are due for his contribution to Andreas Heine, as the leader of the McKinsey project team.

Finally, we would have found it impossible to make a simple book out of this wealth of material without the editorial support of Christel Delker and Marianne Denk-Helmond, who helped edit the original German book; Helen Robertson, who translated the book; and Partha Bose and Robert Whiting, who edited the book in English. Our special thanks are also due to Paula Duffy, Carol Franco, Caitlin Deinard, and the team at the Harvard Business School Press.

We would like to say a very warm thank you to all these contributors—and hope that simplicity will keep helping them to win in the future.

October 1994

SIMPLICITY WINS

INTRODUCTION

✦ ✦ ✦ ✦ ✦ ✦ ✦ ✦ ✦ ✦ ✦ ✦

Excellent Performance
and Simplicity

*I*N the five years between 1985 and 1989, sales of many German machinery manufacturers grew only half as fast as the gross national product (GNP), yielding meager returns of less than 3 percent. But in the same period, some competitors achieved growth rates of 9 percent, far outstripping the 5 percent growth rate in GNP, to produce an average yield of 7.4 percent.

This was just one of the findings of a broad-based industry survey conducted by McKinsey & Company in collaboration with the Technical University in Darmstadt. The survey of 39 companies in two related industries—mechanical engineering (including machine-tool and textile machinery builders, and white goods makers) and component manufacture—showed that, surprisingly, excellent results were clearly linked to above-average simplicity and rigorous implementation of that principle in strategic and operational management.

The analysis uncovered this success pattern in the "boom" period of 1985–1989; it was seen again in the recession that we have experienced since 1990. Although the average return on sales of the segment fell from 8 percent in 1989 to about 2 percent in 1991, the "simple" companies still had a return on sales three times higher than firms afflicted with over-complexity. Moreover, the successful companies were able to widen their lead in labor productivity from about 20 percent to 25 percent. Analysis of the companies with the best performance in both return on sales and productivity showed them to be much simpler, in terms of product range and customer structure, vertical integration and number of suppliers, concentrated focus of R&D investment, logistics and location structure, investment in systems, or entrepreneurial organizational structure.

The survey findings reaffirmed the fact that there is no such thing as a "bad" industry, and that successful companies, even in "problem" industries and "difficult" times, can be much more successful than bad ones in thriving, future-oriented businesses. The findings also provided a blueprint for the route to superior performance: simple goals, structures, and procedures, selected and designed without compromise, and rigorously implemented. Moreover, this notion of simplicity has a great deal to do with selectivity and concentration of effort, little to do with downsizing, and nothing at all to do with corporate anorexia.

That it is far less important which industry you compete in than how you compete is good news—not only for the German machinery industry, which, after a brief recovery in the early 1990s, is back in trouble again, but for any industry anywhere in the world. The simplicity route can lead companies out of apparently hopeless situations in a wide variety of industries, particularly where cyclical downturns in customers' industries and fierce international competition are restricting their freedom to act.

But this simplicity route is by no means immediately obvious. The urge to add complexity in order to adapt to what the market seems to want and internal pressures dictate is all too ingrained and widespread. Fielding a large army of product variants in the war against market stagnation and falling market share is perhaps the most familiar pattern. But pursuing presumed synergies through enlarged central functions, integrating extensively forward and backward to capture know-how and cost advantages, or—to manage all this—installing increasingly complicated data-processing systems are also common.

Our hypothesis that adding complexity to cope with complexity is a seriously flawed approach was formed over a period of years in many consulting situations in different companies, industries, and countries. We have seen countless indications that, in management as elsewhere, a little effort can go a long way, that restraint is the mark of the master, and that the art of elimination liberates undreamed-of forces.

Among the companies surveyed, the best are growing almost four times as fast as their weakest competitors, and their return on sales is two

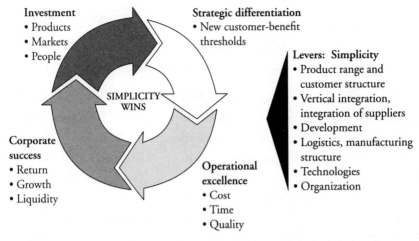

Investment	Strategic differentiation
• Products	• New customer-benefit
• Markets	thresholds
• People	

Levers: Simplicity
- Product range and customer structure
- Vertical integration, integration of suppliers
- Development
- Logistics, manufacturing structure
- Technologies
- Organization

SIMPLICITY WINS

Corporate success
- Return
- Growth
- Liquidity

Operational excellence
- Cost
- Time
- Quality

Simple levers drive a winning wheel of performance and profitability, and ensure future superiority.

Exhibit I-1. The Winning Wheel

and a half-times as high. The successful companies achieve this level of performance because they keep a "winning wheel" turning: they achieve both clear strategic differentiation in value to the customer and operational excellence in cost, time, and quality. This leads to sustainable corporate success, which, in turn, makes possible future-oriented investment in new products, markets, or people—thereby allowing strategic differentiation, and so on (Exhibit I-1).

HOW GOOD IS "GOOD"?

For the purposes of the survey, corporate success was defined by a "performance indicator," which provides a clear comparison of how individual companies stack up against one another in both absolute and relative terms.

Success—including that of companies—has many sources. And it can come in just as many guises: for companies, success can include market share, profit, growth, customer loyalty, financial strength, image, and so on. Real—and sustainable—success will always be a blend of these factors. That was the idea behind the performance indicator used by the survey team as a basis for classifying "successful" and "less successful" companies.

This weighted indicator included figures for return on sales (50 percent), growth (25 percent), and liquidity (25 percent): outstanding results in return on equity and return on sales are essential to enable successful companies to indulge in one of their most important shared characteristics: the propensity to invest. They invest an average of 10 percent of their value added, or some DM16,000 per employee per year—about twice as much as their less successful competitors. Their lead in manufacturing standards (for example, the use of new technologies such as CAD/CAM), product innovation, new market development, and staff training is correspondingly high.

Above-average growth is still an important success factor, despite skepticism about the mania for "gigantism." Growth is the only way to achieve high labor productivity or optimized vertical integration and still meet social goals. This is particularly important in Germany's social market economy—the *soziale Marktwirtschaft*—which aims to achieve a balance among currency stability, satisfactory growth rates, and an optimal level of employment. Even vital injections of new skills and know-how through new hires cannot confer full benefit if there is insufficient growth.

And finally, liquidity, understood in this context as gross cash flow compared to sales, is an absolutely fundamental prerequisite if companies are to have the flexibility to take swift strategic action.

In each of these performance indicators, the successful companies enjoy a very substantial lead over the less successful—ranging from 78 percent in return on equity to 348 percent in nominal sales growth (Exhibit I-2). The results were more widely spread in mechanical engineering than in the apparently more uniform group of component manufacturers. In return on sales, for example, the successful mechanical-engineering companies achieve on average more than five times the figures of less successful companies, while in component manufacturing the difference is only half that. Growth and liquidity both reveal a similar picture.

In both industries, success rests on broad foundations. The leaders do not achieve growth at the expense of earning power; the fastest expanding companies are also the most profitable. And the analysis exploded another common myth about performance improvement: that higher quality and/ or speed are bought at higher cost, and vice versa. Although it is true that the successful companies all have a special strength in one of the factors of cost, time, or quality, they are also better than the less successful companies in all three dimensions.

The most striking similarity among the top performers is that they

+ Are superior in cost, time, and quality simultaneously—and have a clear-cut competitive lead in one of these three dimensions of operating performance.

+ Adhere to the one key principle: uncompromising simplicity, in terms of the objectives they set and of the structures and procedures they employ to achieve them.

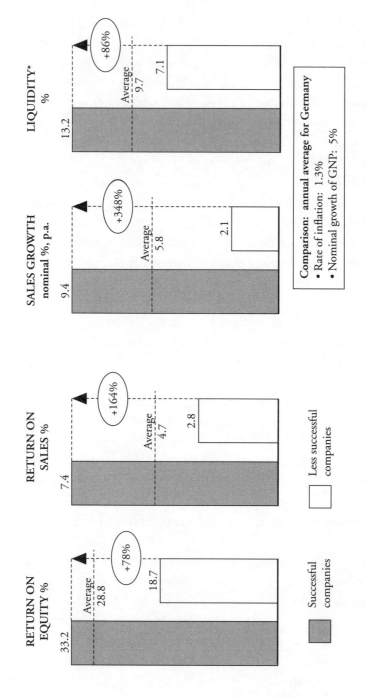

RETURN ON EQUITY %

33.2

Average 28.8

+78%

18.7

RETURN ON SALES %

7.4

Average 4.7

+164%

2.8

SALES GROWTH nominal %, p.a.

9.4

Average 5.8

+348%

2.1

LIQUIDITY* %

13.2

Average 9.7

+86%

7.1

Comparison: annual average for Germany
- Rate of inflation: 1.3%
- Nominal growth of GNP: 5%

Successful companies

Less successful companies

*Gross cashflow/sales

Successful companies have an impressive lead in all the performance indicators.

Exhibit I-2. Machinery and Component Manufacturers, 1985–1989

SUPERIOR IN COST, TIME, AND QUALITY

The survey quantified the cost, time, and quality lead enjoyed by the successful machinery manufacturers. Compared with their slower-growing, lower-earning competitors over the five-year period of the survey, the cost efficiency of the successful companies, expressed as value added per employee, amounted to DM119,000 (as against DM99,000); in terms of time, they achieved an average production throughput time of about eight weeks (half that of the less successful); and, on the quality front, two-thirds of their products were superior to those of competitors, as against one-quarter for the weaker manufacturers (Exhibit I-3). Similar ratios distinguish the successful from the less successful component manufacturers.

Focus

Despite this all-round superiority, the decisive competitive advantage held by the successful companies is always clearly focused on one of the three dimensions. Machinery manufacturers are finding it increasingly difficult to differentiate themselves on the time dimension, since the throughput times of all the successful companies are now much shorter than those of the less successful. On the quality dimension, however, some companies in the leading group have twice as high a percentage of superior products as even their closest competitor, and are up to 100 percent better than the less successful in cost efficiency. In these cases, the use of higher quality or lower costs to achieve strategic differentiation in the market is unmistakable (Exhibit I-4).

For the component manufacturers, although product quality is the sine qua non of success, it no longer provides opportunities for differentiation, since all the successful companies offer comparable, high-quality products. Opportunities do exist, however, in time and cost. One company in the leading group needs only one-third of the throughput time of weaker competitors, and another achieves double the productivity per employee.

Resource Deployment

Even more important than superior overall efficiency is the structure of resource deployment. The best among machinery and component manu-

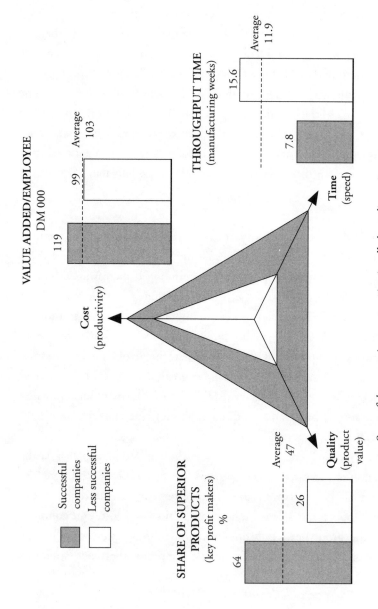

Succesful companies are superior in all three dimensions.

Exhibit I-3. Machinery Manufacturers, 1985–1989

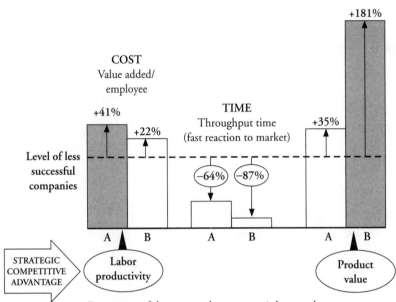

Every successful company has one special strength.

Exhibit I-4. Performance Rankings of Two Successful Machinery Manufacturers

facturers alike understand that those functions and activities that are critical to success must be provided with the resources their importance demands.

Relative to value added, the most successful machinery manufacturers need only slightly more than half the number of R&D employees required by their weaker competitors, and about two-thirds the staff in purchasing and logistics, production, and administration. In sales, marketing, and service, however, the more successful companies have 80 percent more staff than the less successful (Exhibit I-5). Precisely because of their better productivity in the other functions, they can afford to devote more highly concentrated energy to working the market.

The best component manufacturers follow a different principle. Here, the overriding condition for success is to ensure maximum quality at lowest possible cost. From 1985 to 1989, component makers' highest productivity increases were in production (20 percent) and, above all, in sales and

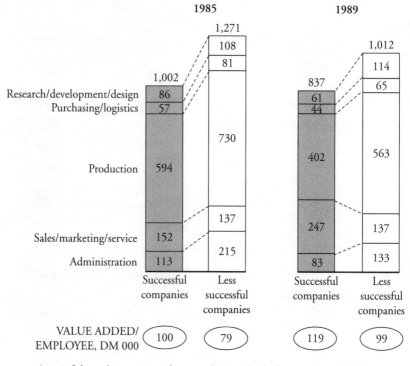

Successful machinery manufacturers have a lead of more than 20% in labor productivity.

Exhibit I-5. Number of Employees Per DM100 Million of Value Added

marketing (65 percent). Today, the most successful component makers have one-fifth of the employees required by the less successful.

UNCOMPROMISING SIMPLICITY

Everything points to the fact that the superior performance of the leading companies—as measured by growth, return on sales, and liquidity—is attributable to simplicity and rigorous implementation: simple, realistic objectives and a high rate of realization, achieved through simplicity in structures and procedures. This pattern recurs without exception in all functions of the business system, from cooperation with suppliers through purchasing, development, and production to sales and service.

Simplicity in setting and achieving realistic objectives is clearly demonstrated by the increase in productivity per employee achieved through automation. The successful machinery manufacturers aimed to increase productivity by 18 percent, while the less successful aimed higher at 21 percent. Five years later, the successful companies had achieved a 29 percent increase in employee productivity, far exceeding their target, while the less successful had achieved 19 percent, falling short of their aim. Simplicity in structures and procedures expresses itself in such approaches as decentralization of responsibilities, or concentrating on labor productivity, rather than maximizing every last detail of machine productivity.

But if, as our experience and the survey analysis suggest, excellent performance in cost, time, and quality comes mainly from simple objectives and rigorous implementation, where do these strengths come from in the first place? How are simple, realistic, implementable goals, and the high-impact simple structures and procedures formed and developed?

The crucial behavior pattern covers the entire spectrum of strategic and operational management activity. It is seen, for example, in simplification through strategic concentration—on distinctive customer value and on those stages of the value-added chain where a company is particularly strong. It is also seen in simplification of interfaces, both internal and external: externally, reducing the number of customers and suppliers and optimizing interaction with them; internally, crossing—or "blurring"— functional boundaries. And finally, it is seen in clear, transparent procedures for managing in-house complexity, based on simple goals with direct relevance to business performance.

WHAT ARE THE LEVERS?

The survey identified a number of levers by which the successful companies achieved superior results through simple solutions. The levers that these companies apply in designing, implementing, and continually improving their ingeniously simple objectives, structures, and procedures are available to the top management team of any company:

+ Product range and customer structure: concentrate on volume segments, and core customers and core products offering optimum customer value.

+ Vertical integration: capitalize on areas where the company is strong by expanding vertical integration; otherwise, when outsourcing, reduce number of suppliers and integrate them better.

+ Development: increase downstream development efficiency by reducing risk upstream, and innovate in small, rapid steps.

+ Location structure and logistics: configure locations around products—with dedicated plants or "plants within plants"—and optimize materials flow.

+ Technology: simplify engineering before automating.

+ Organization: ensure transparent, simplified, decentralized structures, and create entrepreneurial spirit.

Product Range and Customer Structure: Concentrating on Core Areas and Delivering Optimum Customer Value

Simplicity is nowhere more conspicuous than in the portfolio of the successful companies' products and customers. For machinery manufacturers, limiting product-range variety makes a decisive difference in return on sales: companies that restrict product variety achieve returns of about 7 percent; competitors with greater product variety, only about 4 percent. Among component manufacturers, return on sales is decisively influenced not only by limiting the number of types of parts used in production, but also by focusing on a narrower range of customers. Component manufacturers that vigorously restrict both customer and part variety achieve returns on sales of about 7 percent, against 3 percent for those that do not, and 4 to 5 percent for those that restrict only one.

Nevertheless, the survey made it equally clear that success through simplicity is not a matter of "simply" dropping products, parts, or customers. What is necessary is skillful standardization, targeted selection of areas of emphasis, concentration on clear customer value, and finally—for manufacturers of machinery and components alike—superior competitiveness in core segments.

Streamlined product range: Successful machinery manufacturers—producing machine tools, construction equipment, or printing presses—require only 20 to 30 percent of the number of product groups to achieve the same level of sales as their less successful counterparts in the same segment. Where these successful companies build customized products, they delay final specification—the "freeze point"—to as late a stage in production as possible, which gives them larger lot sizes to work with in parts manufacturing (some 60 percent larger than those common among their less successful competitors) and a smaller number of types of parts and components to cope with in the assembly phase.

What allows these successful companies to postpone the freeze point is their shrewd use of modular designs and interchangeable parts; standard products are modified into customer-specific solutions during the final stages of assembly. These companies are setting a kind of industry standard with their products that puts them a cut above the rest in all three dimensions of production strategy—cost, time, and quality.

Fewer parts, fewer customers: Successful component manufacturers also need only about 30 percent of the product range of their less successful competitors to achieve the same sales. They too have larger lot sizes in parts production. Where the pattern of success differs between them and machinery manufacturers is their higher share of low-volume C products and a much earlier freeze point. Both differences spring from differences in customer structure.

For the same sales, successful component manufacturers need only about one-tenth as many customers as their less successful competitors in comparable segments. This means they very systematically limit their range of customers, servicing the truly core segments with high-volume requirements. Naturally, they are forced to carry some marginal product lines to cater to core customers' needs. (No automotive components supplier, for instance, could offer an OEM customer only A products and refer that customer to the competition for C products.)

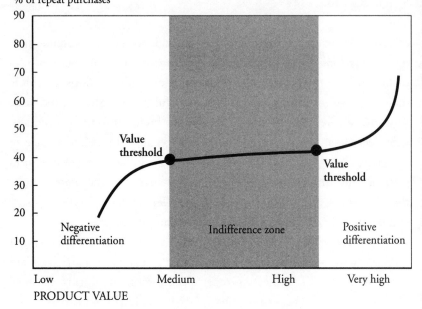

CUSTOMER LOYALTY
% of repeat purchases

Only extreme differences in product value influence customers' interest.

Exhibit I-6. The Indifference Zone

Even so, successful component suppliers have found it worthwhile to set up dedicated production lines and optimize individual products to cover core customers' needs. Therefore, the freeze point for the customer-specific configuration can be relatively early.

Clear customer value: In optimizing customer value, which is the core of success for both types of company, the concept of the "breakpoint"—the value or performance threshold—plays a decisive role. The successful companies do not aim for any and every improvement in their product offerings, but for those improvements that take them across a value threshold in the eyes of the customer (Exhibit I-6).

A classic example is the reduction in film development time. When a customer had to wait five days, a reduction to three days made little difference. But a value threshold was crossed when photos were ready within an hour. In department stores and shopping malls with film developing facilities, customers enthusiastically welcomed the opportunity to hand in their films before shopping, and collect the finished prints before leaving the store or mall.

The day of the mini-labs had arrived: the combination of convenient location and drastic time reduction soon won them considerable market shares. Latest analyses have shown that such value thresholds are moving targets: the next is probably 10 minutes, since more and more customers would like to get their prints immediately.

Rigorous implementation: Many of the success factors touched on above have also been recognized by the less successful component and machinery manufacturers. What holds the weaker companies back in both industries is primarily an inability to follow through on their objectives. For instance, successful companies are much more hard-headed about dropping "shelf-warmers." As a percentage of production, top companies discontinue about twice as many slow items every year as their less successful competitors—although the latter also claim to consider variety reduction an important goal. By the same token, all companies know that the profitability of serving marginal customers has to be eyed critically. But successful companies cross C customers off their lists; less successful companies find "strategic reasons" for continuing to serve them.

All competitors are familiar with the well-established principle that larger lot sizes generally lead to cost savings. However, successful companies create separate production lines for high-volume products, removing the more "exotic" items and spare parts production to other departments so that they do not put a drag on the learning curve in the high-volume sector. Less successful companies shy away from such compartmentalization in the belief that separate production of low-volume products and spares is more expensive and leads to idle capacity on the high-volume production lines.

Vertical Integration:
Building On In-House Strengths and Integrating Key Suppliers

Advocates of a low degree of vertical integration usually claim that it makes fixed costs variable, so that if demand declines they are not immediately threatened by a precipitous drop in earnings. However, by no means all the successful machinery manufacturers keep their degree of vertical integration particularly low, and among component manufacturers, the best usually produce an even higher proportion of the value added in-house than their less successful competitors. The leading companies are convinced that merely pushing the cost problem outside is not the whole answer, and prefer to invest in stable supplier relationships, explicitly designed to benefit both parties.

The approaches these companies have developed are invariably grounded in simplicity: the share of value added they retain in-house is geared to making the most effective use of the company's core strengths; the choice of suppliers is guided by considerations of quality rather than quantity; and relationships with suppliers are based on partnership rather than confrontation.

Leveraging core strengths: Successful machinery manufacturers retain manufacturing stages in-house only where they are operationally superior. Where they are weak or have low labor productivity, they use outside suppliers and achieve differentiation through better systems design and integration. Less successful companies either manufacture almost everything in-house despite operational weaknesses, or contract out a broad range of production operations, even when they are capable of doing them efficiently themselves.

Among component manufacturers, the more successful companies typically have greater vertical integration than the less successful. However, that does not mean that high vertical integration is the key to success. Rather, the successful companies have achieved their market position by virtue of their operational strengths. In a market in which product design and systems concepts are becoming more and more alike, operational strengths offer the best opportunities for differentiation.

In deciding which operations to outsource, top management in the successful companies specifies broad—but quantified—objectives regarding vertical integration, based on the company's strategic objectives. The less successful companies rely on detailed make-or-buy instructions and rules for each sector within the company. They also often leave the decision to functions such as production, whose self-interest makes them wholly unsuited to the task.

Specialized outside suppliers can have a wage cost advantage of up to 40 percent and it can often make good sense to outsource noncritical components that offer no opportunity for technological differentiation. But even those manufacturers that systematically benefit from individual cost advantages of suppliers often neglect overall optimization. The in-house design engineer drawing up blueprints for manufacture-to-design rarely has sufficiently detailed knowledge of the optimization possibilities available in production and can easily overlook design-to-cost potential on the order of 10 to 15 percent. Moreover, high transaction costs are often incurred through the frequent interactions needed for specification, control and supervision, and coordination.

Fewer suppliers: The successful companies have from one-half to two-thirds fewer suppliers than the successful companies. Especially for identical parts, the successful companies usually rely on a single supplier that can exploit great economies of scale, whereas the less successful companies tend to play off several suppliers against one another to avoid any dependence on one (Exhibit I-7) and to get better prices. However, these companies fail to recognize what they should know from their own role as suppliers: that single-source suppliers seldom overcharge their core customers, as long as they don't have a monopoly over the technology know-how on which the parts are based. In any case, suppliers should not be chosen on the basis of price. A more relevant criterion is: What technological advantages can the supplier pass on to the manufacturer?

The most effective means of reducing the number of suppliers is to move away from purchasing components manufactured to blueprints to contracting out the production of complete subassemblies or modules. For single sourcing to be successful, however, it is essential to retain sufficient expertise and know-how in-house to be in a position to take advantage of technical progress and continually improve both the function and cost of the bought-in modules in discussion with the supplier.

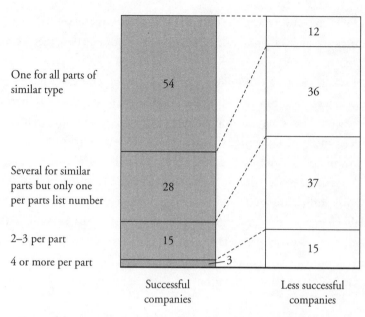

	Successful companies	Less successful companies
One for all parts of similar type	54	12 / 36
Several for similar parts but only one per parts list number	28	37
2–3 per part	15	15
4 or more per part	3	

Successful companies keep it simple and have fewer suppliers per part.

Exhibit I-7. Number of Suppliers (% of sourcing volume)

Closer cooperation: A greatly reduced number of suppliers enables closer cooperation with each, but requires a subtle balance of delegating responsibility and systematically checking that objectives are being met. Of the successful component manufacturers, 67 percent had concluded skeleton agreements with their suppliers, as against only 6 percent of the less successful. Of the successful machinery manufacturers, 55 percent have a systematic supplier-rating system, as against only 40 percent of the less successful.

This new form of partner-like cooperation makes greater demands on both manufacturers and suppliers. Suppliers have to learn to fully exploit the design-to-cost potential in their own development work and to design subsystems on their own. Manufacturers' purchasing departments need to be technical experts, that understand cost structures and are able to judge the technical state of the art. They must evolve into partners of the suppliers and, within their own organizations, establish teams capable of counseling suppliers on questions of rationalization and efficiency.

Development:
Minimizing Risk through Efficient
Upstream Functions and Integration

The most successful machinery and component manufacturers were able to earn good profits even in price-sensitive, high-volume segments. This was in no small measure due to their development departments, which systematically create products for the chosen market segment, and consistently resist the temptation to incorporate extra performance features that are not valued by the customer. But striking advantages in cost, time, and quality can only be achieved when disciplined adherence to goals is combined with optimized development procedures.

Top companies minimize product risks upstream by means of an intensive predevelopment phase. Having thus gained a better overview of the work to be done downstream, they efficiently implement the development of new products. This procedure is supported by a simple organization: development departments are usually structured around product groups or components, which is better than organizing by function as many weaker firms do because there are fewer interfaces to contend with. Know-how transfer within the organization is ensured by means of targeted job rotation.

Upstream risk reduction: Customer requirements—the most important source of new-product ideas—are used by successful companies as early as the initial concept phase. Other sources of inspiration are cooperation agreements and scientific or technical conferences. The less successful manufacturers rely instead mainly on observing competitors, on analyzing patents, and on studying the technical literature. Their early contact with the customer enables leading companies to eliminate, way upstream, those potential products or product features for which there is little demand. Further, they do not specify all details of a product at the start of development, but restrict detailed specifications to those product features that have a long development lead time, and avoid specifying details that are likely to be changed later on. As a result, the successful companies' specifications run to an average of 6 pages, while those of the less successful average 20 pages.

Both successful and less successful companies spend about 11 percent of their development budget on outside development work. But whereas eight out of ten of the successful companies decide specifications jointly with the supplier and have regular consultation meetings, bringing the supplier's full expertise and know-how to bear, only half of the less successful companies rely on joint teamwork. The successful companies devote about 16 percent of total development spending to predevelopment work, against their less successful competitors' 12 percent, which reduces upstream risk and makes downstream development easier and more readily manageable.

Efficiency in downstream development: For products that go through to the main development phase, the successful companies make frequent small incremental improvements in product value at varying intervals, to produce an almost continual stream of innovations and enhancements, all perceptible to the customer. This approach gives them a better idea of whether a given product can be further developed at acceptable R&D costs on the basis of its existing technology, or whether it is necessary to change to a new technology—for instance, from electromechanics to electronics. Companies that aim to achieve major advances in product features at long intervals are often too late in recognizing that a particular technology has reached the end of its potential and are not seen as progressive and forward-looking when competitors offer a more attractive product over a long period. Such companies, taking high leaps in innovation, expose themselves not only to much higher additional complexity but also to much higher risk.

Success with the tactics of small, rapid steps depends on recognizing the different life cycles of different product components and taking them into account in scheduled innovations. The life cycle of a car body design, for example, is likely to be shorter than that of an engine. A further requirement is flexibility during the product launch phase, which can be achieved, for instance, through shorter setup times on machines and by performing trial runs of the new products on the production lines.

The machinery manufacturers set standards during the product development stage; subsequent variants modified to suit a particular customer tend to be the exception. For the successful companies, modifications for a particular customer represent only 13 percent of total development costs, as against 16 percent for the less successful companies. To keep development and product costs in the main phase as low as possible, almost half of the successful machinery manufacturers also apply value-engineering methods and systematically investigate the cost/benefit ratio of every product specification. The less successful manufacturers either omit specifications and thus reduce customer benefit, or rework the design unsystematically to find a low-cost solution, which, while not guaranteeing success, does guarantee delays in launching the product.

The successful companies in both industries spend 35 percent less as a percentage of sales on product development than their less successful competitors. Yet, thanks to their lean product range, they still have almost 40 percent more funds available per product per year. And, with half the development time, they come out clearly superior to competitors in six out of ten of their products, against only three out of ten for the less successful.

Logistics:
Simplicity through Differentiation

The best machinery manufacturers take on average just eight weeks from receiving an order to delivering the product; less successful manufacturers need twice as long. For component manufacturers the timespans are shorter but the relationship is the same.

Successful companies do not buy their way up to this higher level of service at the price of exorbitant logistics costs. Indeed, they have cost levels lower than those of their competitors, requiring up to one-third fewer personnel in such functions as purchasing, flow management, and warehousing. It is precisely because of their short throughput times, coupled with lower inventories, that they do not need to plan over unmanageably long timespans. A time horizon of four months for rough production planning, against the eight-month planning horizon of weaker companies, allows successful companies a much higher degree of flexibility.

This double advantage—better service and lower logistics costs—results in part from the successful companies' streamlined product programs and very compact supplier structures. But a key factor contributing to their superiority is their ability to set up a simple, product-oriented location structure and, within each location, set the right priorities for managing material flows.

Product-oriented plant location: The shortest paths for information and materials flow are achieved by systematically concentrating all functions for a particular product—from development through final assembly—at a single plant. The successful manufacturers establish a single location for each product or product group; the less successful still mostly favor multiple small-plant locations. Top companies will also readily expand on a greenfield site if the labor market, growth, or an extension of the product line requires it. One-half of all the successful manufacturers have at some time built a new plant, as against only one-tenth of the less successful manufacturers. Of the weaker companies, 70 percent are compelled to remain at their traditional production locations, often as a result of declining growth.

Within their product-oriented plant locations, old or new, the successful companies also strive to keep structures simple and transparent. The individual operation becomes a "plant within a plant," not only through systematic matching of production technology to specific products, but also, more important, by adapting planning processes and control systems to the specific production task. One location can then contain plants for both high-volume production of A parts and single-unit production of C parts. Job scheduling for volume production can be as precise as possible, with production equipment and steps optimized to minimize unit costs. In the single-unit operation, rough man-hour standards suffice in place of exact scheduling, expensive equipment is not purchased, and production control is based on rough figures for safety stock levels. Thus, the two operations run on totally different production philosophies, each focused on its particular task.

Clear control priorities: Successful machinery manufacturers have distinct priorities in purchasing, in respect of A versus C parts. For A parts, with high stock turnover and high material value, they aim to keep inventory costs as low as possible, ordering deliveries weekly, in some cases even daily, and, because of the high frequency of orders, stocking no more than a 20-day requirement. For low-cost, low-turnover C parts, they aim to reduce processing costs in materials management, receiving, and warehousing: they deliberately hold relatively large stocks of C parts (up to 181 working days' needs), which means somewhat higher capital tie-up and warehouse space, but lower handling costs and less risk of stock-outs, which can entail high consequential costs. In the less successful companies, differentiation between A and C parts inventories is much less pronounced. In the absence of priorities, however, the materials flows manager is perpetually trying to reconcile ordering costs, inventory costs, and the risk of stock-outs for the entire parts catalog.

Similar differences in approach between the successful and less successful companies are found in the production process, where the key to rapid throughputs is strict adherence to scheduled job sequences. The successful machinery manufacturers ensure this by keeping working stocks of parts at each machine as low as possible and by strictly controlling assembly. They tightly limit the stock of incoming work at the machine to only two working days' lead and ensure compliance with the planned job sequence and throughput times. Under these conditions, the two days' stock allows enough flexibility for necessary modifications to reduce setup time, or undertake maintenance work. The less successful machinery manufacturers hold an average of 22 working days' stock of material at the machine, eleven times as much as the successful companies. This can easily tempt machine operators to optimize the prescribed job sequence according to their own criteria, such as ease of setup. Cumulated over several production steps, this may seriously delay delivery.

Technology: Simplification before Automation

Total automation at any price—trying to control high complexity with sophisticated systems—is counterproductive. Successful companies therefore simplify their structures and procedures before introducing computer-aided technologies. However, as Japanese fully automated "pilot" factories have demonstrated, one decisive principle of success in the use of so-called

C (computer) technologies is to start early. The successful German machinery and component manufacturers have been using C technologies intensively since the early 1980s. By experimenting at an early stage and gaining a thorough understanding of the applications spectrum of systems like CAD, CAE, CAM, and CIM, they were able to target investments in new technologies and deploy them for maximum benefit at markedly lower systems cost. Their spending on computer support is less than half that of their less successful competitors.

The best machinery and component manufacturers in our survey have, since 1985, achieved improvements of about 30 to 40 percent in all three dimensions of cost, time, and quality through systematic use of technologies alone. In the same period, their less successful competitors achieved improvements of, at best, 15 percent.

Selective investment: The successful companies are selective in making their investment decisions, with 40 percent fewer shopfloor data-collection systems installed than the less successful companies. Yet the systems they have report 40 percent more orders back to production control than those of the less successful manufacturers that have invested in hardware they scarcely use. Selective investment can also mean spending very heavily on really promising applications. Six out of ten leading companies, for example, have equipped 60 percent of their development and design staff with CAD, a level achieved by only one in four of their less successful competitors. This effort has led to markedly higher increases in productivity, although that is not the primary indicator of the success of CAD.

Similar differences can be seen in the production of parts. The successful machinery manufacturers now run three-quarters of their machine hours on NC and CNC machines, as compared with only one-third of the less successful manufacturers. The results speak for themselves: the gap in productivity between weaker and stronger companies, which was "only" 20 percent in 1985, has since widened to about 40 percent. An interesting point is that the leading companies, in contrast to conventional wisdom, do not primarily aim at bringing flexibility to rigidly automated plant operations such as transfer lines; instead, they attach much more importance to fully exploiting the potential for automating conventional single-machine production.

Simple structures and procedures: Many companies mistakenly accept an ever-increasing degree of complexity in systems and procedures on the grounds that technical progress has now made complexity manageable. The successful companies take a different tack: instead of using C technologies to retain control of highly complex operations, they use them more efficiently to handle simple, clearly structured tasks. They achieve this by making product designs and, above all, procedures as simple as possible, investing massively in CAD systems, for instance, only after they have succeeded in largely standardizing their products. Machinery manufacturers that first achieve a high degree of product standardization and then expand their CAD facilities are markedly more successful than those that attempt to automate a chaotic operation.

The successful companies also give priority to simplicity in those cases where a complex solution would at first sight appear justified. Although conventional wisdom holds that an integrated systems solution and fully integrated process chains are preferable to "insular" solutions, the successful companies aim first at fully equipping individual departments with systems support. This reflects their ability to define systems architectures within their DP environments in a way that permits their subsequent integration. A particular strength is that they delegate responsibility for the use of C technologies to their operating departments. This enables each function to employ those technologies that promise to yield the highest benefits, and gives the decentralized units the opportunity to optimize their systems in their own way.

The Japanese machine-tool builder Yamazaki is perhaps the perfect example of automation following simplification. The company installed a flexible manufacturing system (FMS) in its factory, halving the number of machines. Core manufacturing then consisted of several machine centers of the same type with fewer than 90 standardized tools. CAD/CAM software was installed for this highly simplified production.

In this case, standardization did not mean modular product design with one optimized building-block for *all* machine tools, or at least a high proportion of identical parts. It was the manufacturing technology that was standardized. The CAD system contains information about the availability of suitable technologies, geometries, and tools. The design engineer finds out from the CAD system if a certain part can be manufactured in the FMS. If it cannot, the design is modified until the technical requirements are met. Once production is feasible, the NC programs are written immediately, and production can start as soon as the materials are available.

Yamazaki made enormous reductions in new-product introduction times by this means—from five to less than two years—and was able to design products with the "technical" skills of the FMS in mind. This optimum product/process fit also allowed a reduction in manufacturing costs of 13 percent, and led, specifically in the United States, to new competitive dynamics because of the shorter innovation times.

Organization:
Transparency and Entrepreneurship

The outstanding performance of the leading machinery and component manufacturers is always supported by their organizational design. This can be explained by a few characteristics that make for simplicity: uncluttered structures, transparency of cause and effect, and rapid feedback of success or failure. This organizational simplicity does not stop at merely avoiding complexity. Here, organization is not primarily a means of creating order, but a way to mobilize creativity and capability by creating self-regulating units that are close to the market, and by fostering employee flexibility and skill building.

Market-oriented, self-regulating units: In contrast to less successful manufacturers, which are usually structured by function, almost 70 percent of the successful companies are organized by product or product group. This clear market orientation, coupled with direct responsibility, engenders entrepreneurial behavior—all the more so, since the principle is also reflected in profit-center (or cost-center) structures throughout all operational departments.

Proper design of organizational structures follows the principle of homogeneous units capable of managing themselves, and upholds the idea of critical operational responsibility. Each unit comprises core activities that belong together and are of decisive importance for corporate success. Thus, in the five years covered by the survey, the successful machinery manufacturers substantially increased their marketing efforts: sales and service teams almost doubled in strength per DM100 million of sales, and service became a profitable, self-financing activity in the market. The less successful companies, by contrast, continued with their old structures.

Over and above formal structures, what makes an essential difference is corporate culture, the value system and style—simply, the way people deal with one another. Leading companies delegate more to decentralized units. For example, the investment budget that second-line managers can decide on their own is four times as large in the successful companies as in the less successful. Matters are discussed and consensus sought in a team, but the responsibilities for implementing and achieving targets lie clearly with single individuals. In the less successful companies, by contrast, such responsibility often rests with a committee or a working group.

Employee qualification and flexibility: The leading companies are also much better able than the others to build up and develop superior and more capable personnel, a strategic competitive advantage that takes much longer for competitors to catch up with than superiority in products or service. The fact that in recent years technically outstanding German machine-tool products were able to regain leading positions in the face of intense Japanese competition was due in no small measure to a personnel capability-building offensive, excellently backed by organizational measures.

The successful companies invest more than DM800 annually per employee in further education and training, almost four times as much as the less successful. But, although the less successful companies concentrate such spending on top management and second-line managers, in the successful companies it is distributed almost uniformly over all levels of the hierarchy. These companies also train their employees to acquire competence in several different specialties so that they gain broad management know-how. Whereas the less successful companies at best pay lip service to job rotation (fewer than 2 percent of employees get to know several different functions during their careers), in the successful companies almost one-quarter of the qualified development staff have previously worked in production, and vice versa.

It is precisely in the area of all-round training and capability, however, that the leading companies still see much more to be done. Training objectives in Germany are often specialization and in-depth knowledge, but not the many-sided management knowledge necessary for optimizing integrated procedures and functions. It is this kind of integrated working organization that seems to be a strength of the Japanese and a contributory factor in their cost and productivity leads of up to 50 percent. Where in Japan, for example, a single team often performs all functions required on a transfer line, in a typical German firm four different groups of functional specialists are at work, from production (machine operators and setup personnel), quality control, and maintenance.

✦ ✦ ✦

UNDERSTANDABLY, anything that looks like a patent remedy is today likely to be received with a good measure of skepticism. That is perhaps understandable, in the light of general experience and the past record of "management by" methods of every kind. However, the various winning patterns and behavioral styles that emerged from our analyses and observations do allow one generalization: among basically comparable companies, the best performer will be the one that is best at implementing simplicity by strategic concentration, interface management, and procedures for complexity management.

Our survey found that such simplicity is rarely as unsubtle as Columbus's egg or the Gordian knot. Examples of simplicity more often remind us that all evolution in nature is based on three principles—variety, selection, and reproduction. This is the royal road to simplicity, in business as elsewhere.

There is also an old mechanical engineer's saying that the best machines are those with the fewest moving parts. And our final confirmation comes from a quite different quarter. That is, from Antoine de Saint-Exupéry, who declared categorically in *Wind, Sand and Stars:* "Perfection is evidently achieved not when nothing more can be added, but when nothing more can be taken away."

In the following chapters we demonstrate in further detail how the six levers generate this simplicity. In doing so, it is our aim to provide positive reinforcement for leaders in machinery and component manufacture and encouragement to the weaker players in those markets. We also hope to suggest how the levers might be adopted in other manufacturing industries.

1

PRODUCT RANGE AND
CUSTOMER STRUCTURE

✦ ✦ ✦ ✦ ✦ ✦ ✦ ✦ ✦ ✦ ✦ ✦ ✦

*Concentrating on Core Areas and Delivering
Optimum Customer Value*

*I*T is in product range and market coverage that the most frequent and
most serious crimes against the law of simplicity are committed. It is
also where such crimes are perhaps most understandable. Here the apparent advantages of variety are all too obvious; the resulting problems are
too well hidden by the use of traditional cost accounting methods and by
departmentalized thinking.

As far as hard-pressed management is concerned, every new product
variant that wins a few niche customers in a stagnating market adds its
mite to profit contributions and capacity utilization. However, no one
looks at the other side of the equation. Consider a steel manufacturer, for
example. Although specialty long products like customized bars, structures,
and other profiles will provide significantly higher profit contributions per
tonne than can be achieved with standardized, mass-produced long products, their total contribution is a drop in the ocean because of their much
narrower production volumes (Exhibit 1-1).

The temptation to evade mass production's unpalatable cost competition by extending the specialty range makes manufacturers loath to face
up to reality. And the reality often looks like this:

✦ The total market for specialty products is far too small; even large
  market shares will not fill production capacity.

✦ Standard products are constantly being technically upgraded, and
  grabbing positions in what used to be niches.

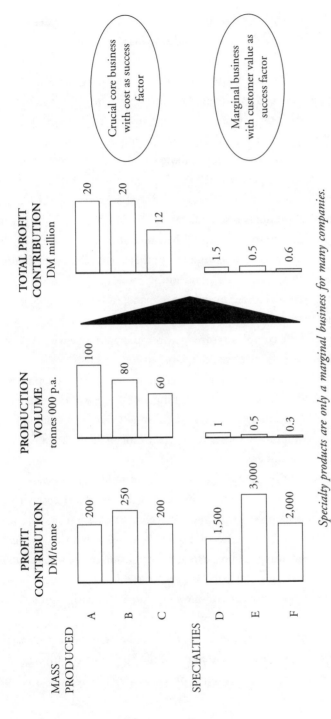

Specialty products are only a marginal business for many companies.

Exhibit 1-1. Mass-Produced and Specialty Steel Products

✦ Niche products bump up the cost of complexity and undermine the competitiveness of the entire product range.

Most companies that boast a specialty-based strategy realize in a few years that they have bogged down. They may have the right infrastructure for specialties; they may have special departments to manage all the ins and outs of product variety; they may have highly sophisticated inspection procedures for every process step, tailored to the needs of the high-tech products. However, what they lack is utilization: for example, steel manufacturers still primarily produce mass-produced steel because the market for specialty steel products is too narrow. Their complicated infrastructure cost them the chance to keep up with competitors that optimized their cost structures in the meantime. As a result, they are stuck in the middle—neither one thing nor the other, and losing money.

How do such incredible mistakes get made? Why can't management identify and remedy the problems early on? The answer lies in lack of transparency. Many complexity-driving decisions are made when it is normally impossible to foresee the knock-on costs.

Consider, for example, the design engineer who needs a certain kind of bolt to make his design work. Designing a new one will only take minutes. He also knows that the weary trek through the parts catalog to see if an existing component meets his specification is likely to mean a lot more work. So he designs a new one. Simple.

The fallacy of this "simple" conclusion can only be appreciated from the right managerial viewpoint. Using an existing bolt will cost virtually nothing in terms of production and service. A new design, on the other hand, will mean an avalanche of expenditure—purchasing, operations planning and scheduling, in-house logistics, inclusion in the service catalog (possibly alongside an older part with the same function), warehousing, and so on. The knock-on costs of one simple item can easily run into four figures.

We don't, of course, mean to imply that the "cheapest" approach is always the best. Consider the extreme case of the Trabant. This legendary little East German car—truly simple in its equipment and accessories and the options available—became practically unsaleable as soon as an alternative was available. And the Trabby is not the only example. However, it is important to bear in mind that simple is not the same thing as old-fashioned or primitive.

Companies that strive to achieve the optimum size and structure for their product range and customer base have to manage a never-ending balancing act between added value and product proliferation. Wrong moves can have a serious impact on profit—such as the 3 or 4 percentage points in forgone return on sales experienced by the machinery and component manufacturers in our study.

The distinguishing feature of the successful companies is simplicity. This is not, however, to be confused with austerity. Our survey showed that it is essential for machinery builders to limit product variety but to pursue a broad customer base. Component makers, on the other hand, with their strong dependence on the special needs of their industrial customers, will make their best profits by selecting customers—as far as possible—in high-volume segments, keeping their customer range as narrow as possible, and giving their core customers the best possible service.

In mastering this balancing act, a company must, on the one hand, avoid the sinking sand of profit-consuming overcomplexity; on the other hand, it cannot neglect highly attractive opportunities for differentiating itself in the market and therefore attracting more profitable business. How is this best achieved? Superior complexity management follows some simple basic rules:

+ Know where and how much—i.e., make both the costs and the benefits of complexity transparent.

+ Think about what is sold and to whom—i.e., carefully consider the choice of products and customers.

+ Make residual variety manageable—i.e., keep internal implementation of the chosen level of complexity as simple as possible.

COST AND BENEFIT:
KNOWING WHERE AND HOW MUCH

As we have seen above, although variety can create value for the customer and open up profit potential, complexity is a significant cost driver. The details of where costs and benefits occur and how large they are must therefore be understood as precisely as possible. For example, a commercial vehicle manufacturer may know that introducing two new product groups will generate 10 percent more sales; it should at the same time, however, be aware that the variety of parts and, accordingly, the cost of complexity will double.

Transparency of both cost and value is thus the first prerequisite for good complexity management. That means knowing exactly what the impact of product and customer variety will be, but also understanding the barriers to clear-sightedness and what actions successful companies take to create the necessary transparency.

Impact of Product and Customer Variety

Looking at the cost side of the equation, our commercial vehicle manufacturer should know, for instance, that no less than 15 percent, and often 20 percent, of an automotive manufacturer's total cost is directly dependent on the complexity of the product range—e.g., on the number of parts and variants. This complexity cost is incurred to varying degrees in a very wide range of functions (Exhibit 1-2). It derives, for example, from preparing drawings, exploding bills of materials, and testing and documentation in research and development, as well as from the number of suppliers required and the scheduling man-hours in sourcing and materials management.

But complexity cost naturally occurs in manufacturing as well, where operations scheduling, machinery setups, machinery and plant usage, tooling up, and floorspace requirements all have an effect. And costs are also incurred by forgoing productivity improvement opportunities, which are far easier to implement in simple production facilities than in complex multifunctional plants. In logistics and administration, too, control work, inventories, transport operations, cost accounting, and stocktaking

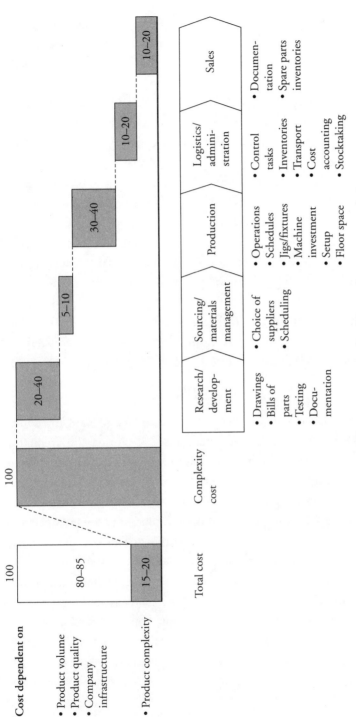

Up to 20 percent of total cost is generated by product range complexity.

Exhibit 1-2. Cost Structure of an Automotive Manufacturer

expenses all grow with rising product complexity and product range variety. And finally, in the sales and service functions, the amount of documentation and levels of spare parts inventories are affected by increased complexity.

But what about the benefit side of variety? Can the new-product groups win new markets, or at least open up new segments? Or is there a risk that the new products will displace the company's existing products? Answering such questions calls for an impartial analysis of the new product groups from the customer's point of view. Will the new products appeal to new customers? Do the new products offer existing and new customers added value for which they are willing to pay higher prices? Or have they just been added to complete the range from a technical or sales perspective?

The costs and benefits of variety should also be understood as they apply to customer range. Commodity manufacturers must often consider the benefits of cutting out the middleman and pocketing the trade margin. And industrial manufacturers with extensive customer networks must look at their high distribution costs from time to time and wonder whether it is really worthwhile to continue servicing their smallest customers.

Systemic Blinkers

What makes the essential cost/benefit transparency so hard to capture? The problem lies primarily in the inadequacy of existing cost accounting systems. The costs of variety are always underestimated because a large portion of the total cost vanishes into overhead. Materials, direct production time, and certain product-specific individual costs are counted as the variable cost of a part or product. But setup times, the costs of operations scheduling, and so on are allocated as overhead. This overallocates costs to mass products and underallocates to specialties.

The benefits of variety, on the other hand, are generally overestimated. Using traditional cost accounting systems, a company finds that hardly a product or customer fails to provide a positive profit contribution. Even the smallest of marginal customers appears at first glance to increase profit. Managers convince themselves that the marginal cost of selling a new product through their already large and powerful sales organization is low;

moreover, processing a customer order seems to cost virtually nothing in this era of IT.

Improving Clear-Sightedness

How can these shortcomings of traditional cost accounting systems be eliminated? One approach might be to install much more refined systems—profit contribution calculations of the first, second, third, and fourth order perhaps? Certainly, in this computer age, that would be possible and might yield a good many useful insights. However, the result would be an extremely complex, cumbersome system that produced questionable results based entirely on historical data ("product A takes up x% of the plant's capacity, product B takes up y%"), was expensive to maintain, and virtually unusable.

We found that the successful companies retain their traditional cost accounting systems, but complement them with periodic observations of complexity cost and benefit based on rules of thumb (e.g., the cost of an ID number, a customer's minimum profit contribution, the cost of processing an order). Moreover, they know how to ensure that the new transparency permeates the organization, so that every decision maker can develop a sound sense of the cost side of complexity.

Armed with rules of thumb, for example, every employee can find out the extra costs of generating additional parts, product features, or processing steps. Our design engineer would have known that having a new bolt included in the product range would cost about DM5,000. A saleswoman would know that throwing business development time and expense at customer XYZ would never make it a core customer, even in the long term, and that she would make better use of her time strengthening relations with the important A customers.

The example of a Japanese washing machine manufacturer illustrates the potential of transparency in variety's cost and benefit. The company's efforts to cover the market as broadly as possible led to a product range of five performance levels (measured by drum size and motor power) with 30 different operating panels. When stubborn profitability problems refused to go away, a cost analysis revealed that the company's manufacturing complexity cost was extremely high. At the same time, an analysis of customer value showed that three types of machine would be enough to meet all needs, and that customers did not want more than three different operating panels. At the top of customers' priorities, by contrast, was differentiated exterior design—for example, for front-panel decor, since cramped living conditions in Japan meant that the washing machine was a piece of furniture that had to harmonize with either the living room or kitchen decor.

The analysis revealed that the company was piling up complexity costs in areas not appreciated by the customer, but was failing to broaden its customer appeal. Once the company had grasped the problem, it was relatively easy to solve. The product lines were completely revamped, and the company gained both significantly higher market share and substantial cost reductions.

PRODUCTS AND CUSTOMERS: THINK ABOUT WHAT IS SOLD AND TO WHOM

Knowing every detail of product and customer variety and being able to attribute the corresponding cost and benefit is one thing. It is a difficult skill to master, and is certainly worth the attention of a high-caliber control function. But it is quite another matter to draw the right conclusions from the findings and implement them consistently over the long term. Responsibility for success here rests with the chief executive. And success means exploiting every opportunity for handling complexity—from rigorous pruning of product and customer variety to deliberate development of variety as a competitive weapon.

Limiting Product Variety

Conspicuously, the successful machinery manufacturers achieve given sales levels with far fewer products than the less successful companies do (Exhibit 1-3). What can we learn from this? What levers do the successful machinery manufacturers use to achieve this masterly leanness?

To begin with, the successful companies have remained competitive

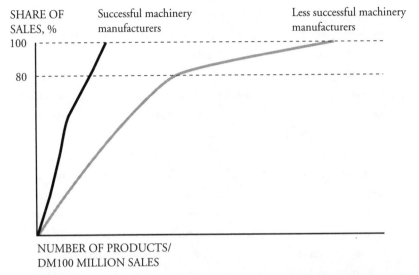

Successful machinery manufacturers concentrate their sales on fewer products.

Exhibit 1-3. ABC Analysis of Product Range

in the volume segment. Not only have they resisted being pushed into niches, they are doing battle with their competitors on the cost side as well. The fact that they managed to increase their already relatively high productivity by close to 20 percent between 1985 and 1989 is clear proof of that.

Second, the successful machinery manufacturers invest significantly more in sales and service. Their aim is not just to take a slice of the attractive service business, but also to limit the complexity of a product range that is—apparently—dictated by the market. Their approach is to channel customers' wishes in a specific direction, by using targeted salesforce management, getting involved early in the customers' decision-making processes, or even influencing the whole market.

The value of this sales and service-oriented approach cannot be overemphasized. Yet three of its elements are still often underestimated:

+ Untargeted use of the salesforce directly increases complexity. Almost any salesperson will be totally confused by the technically possible product variety described in the sales manuals. The only answer is targeted training, which will give the salesforce the skill to steer a customer's interest—without underplaying that customer's needs—toward the company's favored core product range.

This approach is by no means restricted to machinery or component production; it has also been used successfully, for example, by a manufacturer of specialty steel. Despite a market share of 50 percent, the company was unable to achieve any real economies of scale: its customers' additional specifications had fragmented its total volume into more than ten quality subgroups. To complicate matters even further, the reasons for customers' special requirements were many and varied. In some cases, special services had simply come to be taken for granted; in others, process-dependent limitations necessitated specific product characteristics; and in yet other cases, the manufacturer's own account managers wanted to avoid every possible risk by offering additional specifications.

Achieving radical standardization meant eliminating these problems one by one. And to avoid causing problems for customers, the process could only be achieved step by step and relatively slowly. And, of course, customers had to be offered some incentive to relinquish their accustomed specifications or bring their processes in line. The company achieved its goal without price concessions or discounts. Most customers were amenable to the argument that the change would bring tangible advantages in the form of consistent quality and shorter delivery times (reduced from 10 weeks to 2).

✦ For suppliers to the automotive industry, early involvement in the car manufacturers' decision-making process is the key lever for limiting product variety. (The only equally effective tool is concentration on A customers.) Early involvement allows suppliers to seek solutions that best fit their own processes, in-house standards, and parts lists, while fulfilling the OEM's development objectives.

✦ Finally, dominant market players can also choose to simplify their product range by influencing an entire market. Such companies can set standards with their core products, provided they fulfill their customers' basic needs, and also offer attractive compensation for the per-

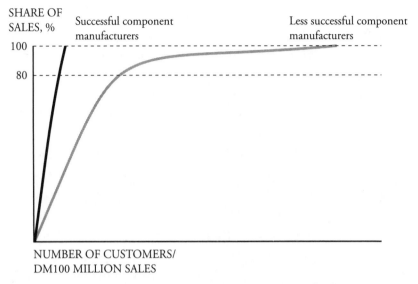

SHARE OF
SALES, %

Successful component
manufacturers

Less successful component
manufacturers

100

80

NUMBER OF CUSTOMERS/
DM100 MILLION SALES

Successful component manufacturers concentrate their sales on far fewer customers.

Exhibit 1-4. ABC Analysis of Customers

ceived loss of value through standardization (superior product features or service). Machinery manufacture reveals some widely known examples, and in component manufacture, too, some famous names have had a decisive impact on the course of the market. For example, IBM set industry standards in hardware in data tape machines; and UNIX and Windows set standards in software.

Limiting Customer Range

Keeping customer range within bounds is perhaps the key step toward profit-boosting business simplification—for automotive industry suppliers, for example. All the successful automotive suppliers in our study concentrated clearly on A customers in the high-volume segment; less successful companies, on the other hand, had a lot of marginal customers (Exhibit 1-4).

An idea of how crucial this focus on A customers is can be formed by an ABC analysis of products and customers. Products can be divided into three categories, depending on their importance to the company: A products—those with high stock turnover and high material value—which form the core assortment (but maybe only 20 percent of the total), and account for approximately 80 percent of sales and profit; B products with a promising future and the prospect of eventually achieving A status; and C products—low-cost, low-turnover products—which are of lesser importance and likely to stay that way.

A similar analysis of customers defines core—or A—customers, which are indispensable to the company; B customers, which can be identified as future key money makers; and C customers, which will never be important to the company because, for example, their sales potential is too low.

The study revealed that successful companies perform such ABC analyses far more often than less successful ones do. Forty percent of the successful machinery manufacturers use the ABC/ABC analysis, whereas only 14 percent of the less successful ones do. The analysis is even more important for the component manufacturers. Here, 80 percent of the successful ones use it, against 75 percent of the less successful ones. Although among component manufacturers there seems to be no great difference between the successful and the less successful in use of the analysis, the difference comes principally from how well they implement their findings. We believe that successful companies have an implementation ratio of two to three times higher than the less successful ones.

The successful component manufacturers, for example, combined the two analyses and found that the major share of their C products went to C customers (Exhibit 1-5). And they were able to act on that information. They realized that C customers were a problem, because even their A requirements are pure C products for the supplier. And the argument that claims that "You can supply a C customer if that customer is prepared to bear the higher costs" should be subjected to close scrutiny. Most companies have never been able to capture completely the actual costs of supplying C customers. It is a different matter if C customers can be served with the same products as A customers; in this way, it is possible to keep the harmful effects of complexity escalation in sales, control, and dispatch within bounds.

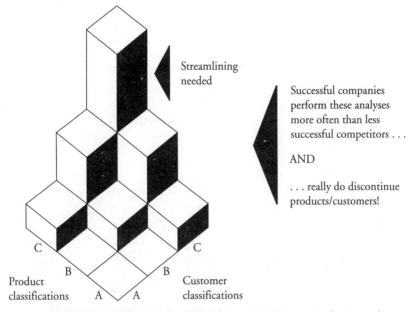

A combined view of the assortment and customer structure indicates costly overcomplexity.

Exhibit 1-5. Classical C Product/C Customer Analysis

Another feature that distinguishes the successful component manufacturers from their less successful competitors is that, virtually as a free spin-off from limiting customer variety, they also gain a much leaner product range (Exhibit 1-6). This is achieved not by trimming the product offering, and running the risk of losing target customers, but by concentrating on A customers in the way outlined above. A customers will be supplied with the products that are important to them, even if some of them are definite C products for the supplier.

Exploiting Variety as a Competitive Weapon

However, variety is not to be avoided out of hand. Not all complexity management consists of restriction and elimination. In certain business situations, possibly even in entire industries, there is more to be achieved from complexity than from rigorous pruning. That is true, for example, where lucrative potential can be developed by servicing certain sales chan-

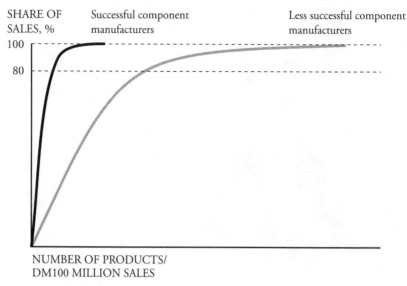

SHARE OF
SALES, %

Successful component
manufacturers

Less successful component
manufacturers

100

80

NUMBER OF PRODUCTS/
DM100 MILLION SALES

Successful component manufacturers concentrate their sales on fewer products.

Exhibit 1-6. ABC Analysis of Product Range

nels, regions, or niches that would be inaccessible to a standardized product offering.

Some companies can close their domestic markets to external competitors by exerting a targeted influence on legal standards or registration regulations. In power switches, for example, a dominant manufacturer in a small country can preempt competitors from outside by persuading government regulatory authorities to standardize according to its product specifications. This does not mean that foreign players are prevented from competing in that market. It does, however, mean that the volume is that of a niche market.

Of course, against the background of global standardization, such a policy drives variety up and, in the light of our discussion above, should be avoided. Clearly, from an individual company's point of view, variety can be seen as a shield against possibly overwhelming external competition. However, it is doubtful how long such a strategy can be sustained in an environment of increasing liberalization.

In some cases, it makes sense to use a special product range to protect certain lucrative sales channels from imitation. This applies, for example, to electric wiring material, which is offered by the wholesale and specialist trade or by installers on the one hand, and by construction markets and do-it-yourself (DIY) stores on the other. A standardized offering would be impossible in these two sales channels with their radically different success factors.

The construction market and DIY stores, with limited selling space holding virtually all the inventory, have no interest in a particularly differentiated assortment. They want to present the consumer with a fast-turning, streamlined product offering at attractive prices. For the wiring manufacturer, this implies a narrow assortment, but also poor prices; the company needs to be competitive as a low-cost supplier.

Achieving sales through wholesalers and the specialist trade or installers, on the other hand, means dealing with a large number of channels. The trade margins alone demand higher end-customer prices, which can only be justified by clear differentiation from the construction market products. Such differentiation is achieved by extreme product range extensions, or even complete separation of the professional and construction market assortments.

Concentration on special segments, too, can be sensible or even desirable in individual cases. This is the case where customers are prepared to pay, for special versions, a premium that is significantly higher than the actual additional cost—in special machinery or machine-tool construction, for example. However, niches where this strategy will pay off over time are not that common. And our study showed clearly that niche operators generally make lower returns than strong volume-segment companies. A niche approach, then, will normally only work out as a complement to a major volume business.

Most niche strategies, however, do not appear to be the result of long-term strategic thinking. Rather, they often come from a manufacturer's realization that it can no longer be a competitive volume player. Retreating in this way, even into lucrative specialties guaranteeing short-term coverage of full cost, all too often bears the risk that the company will succumb to death by inches in a spiral of evasive maneuvers (Exhibit 1-7).

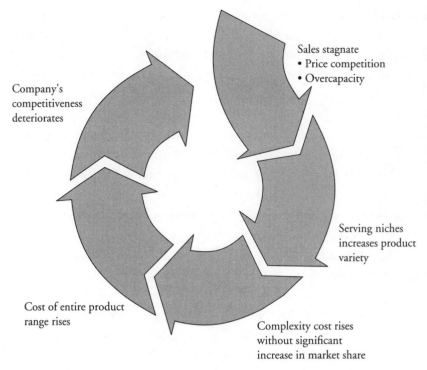

Sales stagnate
• Price competition
• Overcapacity

Company's
competitiveness
deteriorates

Serving niches
increases product
variety

Cost of entire product
range rises

Complexity cost rises
without significant
increase in market share

An exaggerated niche policy starts a vicious circle of complexity and competitive disadvantages.

Exhibit 1-7. The Vicious Circle

RESIDUAL VARIETY MADE MANAGEABLE

Once a company has decided on the right inventory, product range, and customer variety for its market approach, much remains to be done to adapt internally to the chosen level of external complexity. For example, whether the cost/benefit calculations come out right in practice will be decided by the manufacturing stage at which the desired level of product variety is introduced (the freeze point)—in other words, where in the company (or outside it) variety is created.

Shifting the Freeze Point

The availability of differentiated and customer-specific products in the market does not necessarily mean that customer-specific batches have to be made at every stage of production. For example, one telephone manufacturer changed its product structure completely in order to be able to separate the manufacture of housings and electronic parts. As a result, the company could create extreme product variety while using completely standardized internal works, so that complexity affected only part of its production.

Pushing the configuration or freeze point—the stage up to which a product can remain undifferentiated—as far down the line as possible should be the objective of all complexity management. The advantages are evident. Low variety of modules and parts in the early stages makes the famous "batch size of one" and its accompanying expensive automation unnecessary, without having to pay for the privilege with high intermediate storage costs. Further major benefits are significantly higher consistency of quality for standard components and shorter delivery times for orders.

It is important to remember that, if variants are unavoidable, the main focus should be on not allowing variety into the production process until near the end, so as to reduce manufacturing throughput times and keep costs down (Exhibit 1-8).

A special case of targeted freeze-point shifting is the multibrand strategy. If, as discussed above, a company wants to keep dedicated product ranges for special sales channels, there is no need to separate manufacturing as well. The company may be able to meet market requirements simply by changing those external characteristics critical for the purchasing decision at a late stage in the manufacturing process.

Separate Manufacturing

However skillfully a company sets its freeze point, certain parts or components will still have to be made in small or even tiny batches. After all, special and spare parts will always be needed, and in virtually every company they will be part of the core complexity. The real danger lies in falling prey to the illusion of synergy—the idea that small and special batches can be run alongside series production and are an ideal way of filling gaps in capacity utilization.

This is an easy trap to fall into, as one manufacturer of consumer durables found when its assembly line for housing parts was not quite fully

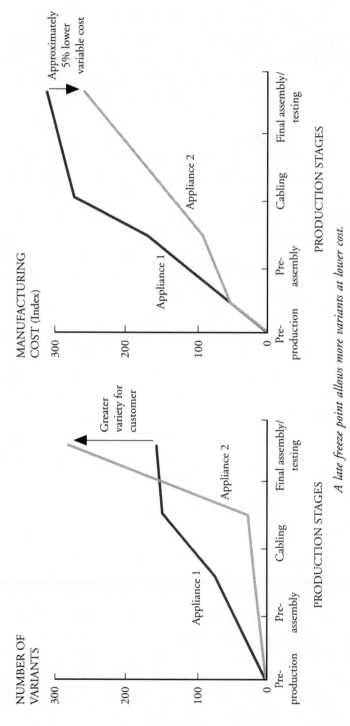

A late freeze point allows more variants at lower cost.

Exhibit 1-8. Variants and Manufacturing Cost in Domestic Appliances

employed. The company decided to make some special products and spare parts on the same line, in addition to three existing mass products. Management realized that this manufacturing mix would lead to additional setup work. However, it was convinced by cost accounting that this effort would be more than compensated for by better utilization rates and the saving of investment in an additional, separate production plant.

It was not until subsequent serious profitability problems arose that management made an intensive competitive comparison. Manufacturing costs proved to be well above those of competitors. And, in contrast to the market leaders, there had been no rationalization in mass products in the five years since the production streams had been merged. The company had been content to minimize setup times instead of exploiting every opportunity to optimize mass production. It had obviously got stuck well short of the optimum point on the learning curve.

This assumption was proved correct once the manufacturing strategy was reversed. The assembly line, once more specializing in three series-produced housings, could be rationalized, and functions such as production scheduling, production control, and materials supply could be radically simplified. Moreover, the control tool could be used much more effectively.

The small series of special products and spare parts that had accounted for about 5 percent of the assembly line's capacity were shifted to shop production. There, the net production time per part was much longer than on the assembly line, but preparatory work, such as operations scheduling, was simplified, as it could be done completely unbureaucratically by the *Meister* (master craftsman) on site.

In short, the additional cost of shop production was well below what could be saved from learning-curve effects for the mass products on the assembly line. And finally, separate production of the special and spare parts allowed for much more accurate cost control, which provided meaningful data as a guide to pricing.

This company's individual experience was entirely confirmed by the results of our comparison of machinery and component makers. Particularly successful companies split up their production far more radically than less successful firms. The reason is that they need a simple, easily manageable manufacturing function that can be optimized at any time for goods produced in large-unit numbers. Experience suggests that they can handle more complicated special assembly more simply by decentralizing it to the *Meister* level. To gain this advantage, they do not seek synergies by using the same parts-assembly aggregates for volume products and specialty products. They optimize labor productivity and, in return, accept slightly lower plant utilization.

Subcontracting Customer Variety

If product variety can be controlled by shifting the freeze point, are there comparable mechanisms for managing excessive customer variety? Indeed there are. There are channels that will undertake the sale and distribution of standardized products. By handling sales of products either without further modification, or with only a limited amount of customer-specific adaptation, trade organizations shield manufacturers from the complexity-driving factor of customer variety.

Such an approach is not only feasible with consumer goods and small commodities. That is proved by Japanese car manufacturers, which look to make batches of 50 to 60 completely identical vehicles in their American transplants. These are passed on in "the standard version" to their sales organizations, where they are then "individualized"—for instance, with special wheel rims or special car radios.

✦   ✦   ✦

NOWHERE IS THE WINNING PRINCIPLE of simplicity, combined with rigorous implementation, so clearly evident as in the management of product range and customer variety. And the improvement potential to be gained by streamlining product ranges and customer structures is correspondingly high. Such improvements come in the form of cost reduction, time gains, and quality improvements; they arise from many sources that produce yields of varying size from company to company.

Slimming down to core products can produce a cost structure that not only boosts returns, but also makes possible substantially stronger growth. Depending on a company's position on the learning curve—and as a rule there is a long way to go—need-based separation of production lines can also reduce manufacturing costs by double-digit percentages. In most cases, a further 20 percent of profit improvement can be gained from shifting the freeze point.

Most companies know what they need to do. Where the weaker companies fail in comparison to the leaders is in not taking a radical enough approach—to strategic concentration, interface management, and the optimization of internal procedures:

+ Strategic concentration has secured the successful companies a strong position in the volume segment. They discontinue twice as many products as less successful competitors—although these, too, normally consider streamlining parts variety to be very important. The leaders drop marginal customers from their customer list, while the less successful companies rationalize why continuing to supply them makes good strategic sense.

+ The successful companies optimize interfaces. They involve suppliers early in the decision-making process, for example; they subcontract some tasks to sales channels; and they eliminate differentiation in as many stages in the manufacturing process as possible (postponing the freeze point).

+ The effect of optimized procedures is demonstrated by successful companies, in separating production lines for high-volume products and "exotics" or spare parts, for example. They maximize labor productivity by decentralizing operational responsibility for special production to the *Meister* level. Less successful companies shy away from the cost of separate manufacturing and seek synergies from adding to capacity utilization in series production.

The period of transition to simpler product lines and customer structures within a company normally takes a whole new-product generation. Experience indicates that the process can take up to five years in the market, depending primarily on the amount of influence the manufacturer can exert on customers' investment decisions.

FURTHER READING

For further discussion of complexity, see Peter Child, Raimund Diederichs, Falk-Hayo Sanders, and Stefan Wisniowski, "SMR Forum: The Management of Complexity," *Sloan Management Review,* Fall 1991, p. 73.

For a more detailed discussion of the freeze point—or order penetration point—see Graham Sharman, "The Rediscovery of Logistics," *Harvard Business Review,* September–October 1984, p. 71.

2

VERTICAL
INTEGRATION

✦ ✦ ✦ ✦ ✦ ✦ ✦ ✦ ✦ ✦ ✦ ✦

Expanding In-House Strengths,
Integrating Key Suppliers

*D*ISCUSSIONS on vertical integration—whether products, parts, or services should be produced in-house or outsourced—often have a way of getting out of hand: Is it really about optimizing the cost structure or about destroying jobs? Is it about making fixed costs variable or about losing know-how? or Is it about gaining flexibility or about plunging into dependence?

Not surprisingly, the make-or-buy debate almost invariably runs into contentious subjective areas. Some see it as the chance to thrust forward into a spectacular high-tech investment. Others see it as a misguided sense of responsibility toward one's own team. Yet objective criteria for a dispassionate and rational decision are not easy to find, nor, when they can be found, are they easy to apply, since almost every case is unique.

However, the good news is that make-or-buy considerations can be expressed in objective terms. What is not such good news is that these considerations have to go further and deeper than is commonly assumed or will be found convenient. To be really useful, changes in the level of integration should make the entire corporate value-added chain more effective, and not just consist of spinning off units or adding on individual machining operations or processes. And when we speak of vertical integration, we include all elements of the chain, not only production.

No amount of observation of prevailing practice in different industries will reveal much about whether high or low vertical integration is a competitive advantage. The question is not even answered by seeing if successful companies in general tend to have less or more vertical integration. For example, our research showed that, in Germany, successful component manufacturers consistently produce more in-house than less successful ones. Yet high vertical integration is not always accompanied by outstanding performance. Among our sample in the machinery manufacturing sector, some of the successful companies had high and some low vertical integration. Looking at other industries, we find that Western automotive manufacturers are traditionally highly integrated, but are now tending to reduce integration; and in plant construction, the most successful companies have very low vertical integration.

Clearly, every company must find its own optimum level of integration. Vertical integration should be used basically to reinforce existing technological and operational effectiveness. Thus, if a company is technologically or operationally superior to its competitors and suppliers, a high level of vertical integration gives it a competitive advantage. If it is weaker, on the other hand, the same vertical integration will be a disadvantage.

Outsourcing to compensate for operational or technological weaknesses is only a good solution if the value-added elements farmed out have nothing to do with what differentiates a company in the market. A component manufacturer, for example, will rarely achieve strategic differentiation with a superior product concept; it is more likely to go for operational excellence, greater economies of scale, a superior process, and a superior logistics function. Companies that increasingly outsource production simply because they are not cost competitive must be prepared to be overtaken by more efficient competitors, or to stand by and watch their suppliers run past them and enter the market in direct competition. Accordingly, excellent component manufacturers are more likely to have high vertical integration than the less successful ones.

Machinery companies, on the other hand, can achieve adequate differentiation with a superior systems architecture or design, with no real need for particular operational strengths. To some extent, they can compensate for operational weaknesses by outsourcing. What differentiates the excellent machinery manufacturers from the poorer performers is that they are a better judge of their competitive position. They typically aim for high vertical integration when they are strong in operations, and tend to out-source their value-added stages when their strength lies in the machine concept/design. It is open to question whether and for how long this principle will remain sustainable. Today many machines become commodities as their life cycles advance, making differentiation possible only through low costs based on operational efficiency. By that time, at the latest, a manufacturer must be in a position to leverage economies of scale and raise its competitive profile through superior performance in operational management.

In some cases, such as the automotive industry, optimizing vertical integration actually means reducing it; only in that way can companies make the significant (and desired) manpower reductions necessary to achieve overall productivity improvements of 30 to 40 percent. At this stage, sociopolitical considerations enter the debate and it is difficult to find a satisfactory answer. But ignoring the issue could well prove fatal, particularly in view of the strength of international competition. Creative solutions are called for. These could include spinning off component manufacturing facilities as independent companies with their own development departments (profit centers), or contracting out entire manufacturing stages to suppliers.

Although reduced vertical integration may not be the cure-all for low operational efficiency, it is just as unrealistic to pretend to be operationally superior in every area. Even outstanding operational management cannot compensate for the negative effects of lost economies of scale and/or high personnel costs.

The successful companies have found a clear line of their own in the muddled make-or-buy debate—one that remains true to the principle of simplicity:

+ Their basic decision on vertical integration considers both technological differentiation and cost optimization.

+ Once they have decided which elements should be outsourced, the excellent companies get cooperation with their suppliers off to a good start with clearly defined systems boundaries and with such trust-building signals as a reduction in the number of suppliers.

+ And finally, they instill throughout their organization the new modes of behavior that make cooperation and change happen, and are, in the long run, the deciding factor in whether the optimization of vertical integration works in day-to-day operations.

THE BASIC DECISION: PROFILE BUILDING AT REASONABLE COST

U.S. manufacturers have gone through phases of thinking that they could differentiate themselves merely through systems concepts and packaging. Having, as a consequence, transferred significant parts of their value-added chain to low-cost countries, they now realize that they have lost sizable parts of their industrial base. Countries they once thought of as no more than cheap supply markets have now overtaken them in the marketplace.

This provides clear macroeconomic confirmation of the power of vertical integration as a reinforcing factor for technological/operational effectiveness. Accordingly, the current revival of some U.S. industries is based heavily on a return to productivity in manufacturing, coupled with in-house value added. In many cases, the Americans are now actually significantly better in this respect than their German competitors, many of which still have to bear the full force of Japanese competition in the future.

The successful companies avoid losing technological/operational effectiveness through simple basic decisions on two key issues. First, on the strategic side, they determine which parts of the value added have to be produced in-house because they are essential to technological differentiation and can also be manufactured more cost-effectively in-house (Exhibit 2-1). They go on, on the cost side, to examine objectively the advantages and disadvantages of producing in-house compared to using efficient suppliers. In doing so, they take an integrated view of costs, one that includes factor costs, scale advantages, productivity, and also—most important— the savings potential in design-to-cost.

Technological Differentiation

The best safeguard to competitiveness is technological differentiation, which offers clear value advantages to the customer. This point must there-

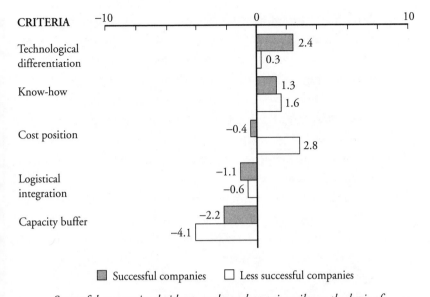

CRITERIA

Technological differentiation — 2.4 / 0.3

Know-how — 1.3 / 1.6

Cost position — −0.4 / 2.8

Logistical integration — −1.1 / −0.6

Capacity buffer — −2.2 / −4.1

▨ Successful companies   ☐ Less successful companies

Successful companies decide on make-or-buy primarily on the basis of technological differentiation.

Exhibit 2-1. Importance to Company of Different Criteria (scalar rankings)

fore be well debated, to determine both whether there are new opportunities for technological differentiation and whether traditional differentiating features are still valid.

A positive example of where technological differentiation has been achieved by bringing new value added in-house is the machine-tool builder Trumpf, which added the development and manufacture of lasers to its program at the beginning of the 1980s.

Trumpf realized the potential of laser cutting very early on, before the industrial exploitation of lasers for machining became widespread. The company had made the decision to outsource hardware and basic software for its control electronics, and to aim for an optimized, tailored system through close cooperation with established control manufacturers. But it saw that the situation was different in laser technology. Here, there were no dominant manufacturers of comparable lasers in the market, and it was obvious that laser-cutting applications for sheet metal—Trumpf's core market—would remain the primary market for this kind of laser for the foreseeable future. Trumpf was thus able to secure a considerable lead over competitors by entering laser technology. In addition, it was sufficiently far-sighted to operate the laser business as a component business as well, so as not to lose out on the economies of scale enjoyed by specialists.

However, caution is required when considering technological differentiation. A company must think about whether the technological advantage will be sustainable or short-lived. Two key questions can determine whether in-house development and production are important or essential for technological differentiation:

1. Does the subsystem or component have a decisive influence on the overall architecture and performance of the product? If so, it is a question of survival for the company to have the know-how and structures to develop and produce the subsystem competitively. Such subsystems, the core components of a product, are "musts" for in-house production or development. Other important subsystems do not necessarily have to be manufactured in-house, although it is critical to retain the development know-how. Here, a manufacturer must be able to have a say in an outside supplier's design, but without destroying the advantages of outsourcing by overspecification.

2. Are there competitive advantages to be won from a technological innovation for the subsystem? In-house development/manufacture should only be considered if the cost and technology advantages can be defended in the long run, as was the case with Trumpf. Typically, this decision means setting up a separate business or profit center which is also free— apart from restrictions on direct competition—to operate in the market and commercialize its products. This approach will work where the funds and management resources to build a strong parallel business are available—and where sufficient economies of scale can still be guaranteed if competitors enter alliances with third parties. Often, however, close cooperation with a good supplier is a better option than going it alone.

Generally speaking, companies must take care not to let the aim of technological differentiation distract them from all else. Differentiation advantages should not carry such a high price tag that they reduce value to the customer overall. When numerical controls were first introduced, for example, many machinery manufacturers tried to produce their own control electronics. But, as basic development costs for controls, and with them the importance of economies of scale in control hardware, increased, these companies found it impossible to produce the controls competitively. Instead of a technology lead, in-house development brought a dramatic competitive disadvantage compared to suppliers, which simply added their own modifications to standard hardware and software.

Optimization of Total Costs

Once the issue of technological differentiation—and whether a given element of the value chain should remain in-house or be outsourced—has been resolved, the question of costs needs to be dealt with. In practice, that often means no more than comparing quoted prices against in-house marginal cost.

Although such an approach may appear to make sense in the short term, it is not the best way to ensure overall optimization of the value-added chain. Price quotations obtained from the market may be loss leaders from suppliers hoping that they can set prices to suit themselves once the customer has reduced its level of integration. In other cases, the prices quoted may be inflated because the suppliers have based their costing solely on existing drawings, without making any allowance for optimization potential. At the same time, they often try to write down any special fixed assets required over a very short period, since they are reluctant to rely long term on nonbinding agreements on order volumes.

Moreover, in-house marginal cost is not an appropriate basis for comparison. When a decision on vertical integration is being taken on strategic grounds, and thus for the long term, it makes a lot more sense to base it on the full cost of production. Yet even the production horizon is far too short: the cost of development and production engineering, among others, should also be taken into account.

Cost optimizers sometimes face opposition from those who claim to argue from a strategic point of view. Their argument holds that the company could push down its break-even point by increasing outsourcing, for which it would be prepared to pay a supplier a sort of "insurance premium." Yet this approach will work only when the supplier is not relying on a constant workload from the partner, but has a real opportunity to fill gaps in orders with demand from other customers. Such opportunities, however, which have always been severely limited, are becoming fewer with the trend toward single sourcing because, in a situation where manufacturers and suppliers are closely tied, the individual customer invariably carries great weight.

Transferring "risk" to the supplier—in extreme cases by sub-contracting demand peaks, while retaining in-house production at constant full utilization—will never produce the desired results. It jeopardizes the trust-based relationship between manufacturer and supplier and prevents the exploitation of other—much greater—potentials, such as design-to-cost opportunities.

Looking beyond dogmatic differences of opinion, which would appear to be unavoidable in view of the perspectives outlined above, the main issue for management is to understand the fundamental cost differences between manufacturer and suppliers. There are four main areas to consider: (1) factor costs, (2) economies of scale, (3) productivity, and (4) design-to-cost potential. This analysis usually produces such unequivocal results that there is no room for dogmatic extremes.

1. Factor costs: Suppliers' factor cost advantages, particularly in personnel costs, can be significant, often too great to be offset by other advantages of in-house production. In the automotive industry, for example, suppliers' personnel costs are typically 30 to 40 percent lower than those of OEMs.

Superficial analysis often shows supplier personnel cost advantages, calculated as annual labor cost per employee, of only 10 to 20 percent. That may well be a relevant figure at the level of the individual employee. A more useful benchmark for a company comparing itself against alternatives, however, is annual labor costs—including such ancillary costs as unemployment insurance—divided by the number of hours worked, giving net labor cost per hour. Since in Germany suppliers' employees often work 1,500 to 1,600 hours per year while OEMs chalk up only 1,100 to 1,300, this calculation typically gives suppliers additional cost advantages of about 20 to 30 percent. Together with the lower annual labor costs per employee, the personnel cost advantage per hour totals 30 to 40 percent.

And for countries with low labor costs, the personnel advantages may be even higher than those illustrated here.

With such significant labor cost advantages available, many manufacturers might consider the make-or-buy issue settled at this point. That, however, would be wrong. Overhasty subcontracting of parts and systems to suppliers can soon lead to substantial cost disadvantages. These can arise when suppliers' skills are inadequate, whether in development, delivery capabilities, or quality. This probably also explains why successful examples of global sourcing have not to date been very widespread. On the one hand, to exploit suppliers' factor cost advantages, a manufacturer must define the technical interface so clearly that there is little need for further coordination. On the other hand, it must play an active role in closing suppliers' know-how gaps.

This route currently offers opportunities for U.S. manufacturers in Mexico and for European manufacturers in some former East Bloc countries that are on their way toward a market economy, such as the Czech Republic or Hungary, and, to a certain extent, Poland. However, such an approach will be successful only if a manufacturer provides funds and management capacity to bring development and production know-how up to Western standards, or if it can induce one of its traditional Western suppliers to provide such "development aid" through a joint venture or a long-term purchasing guarantee.

The attractiveness of low labor costs should not blind companies to the possible attendant risks. Most development departments in these countries are far from world standard, despite a sound technology base. Production facilities are often obsolete and should ideally be replaced with greenfield plants. And management should also bear in mind transportation difficulties (and their impact on JIT), political risks, and, in coming years, rising wages.

2. Economies of scale: Suppliers' scale advantages are often as great as the differences in factor costs. In terms of unit output alone, a supplier will often be in a position to produce on a significantly larger scale. What is often not realized is that there may also be economies of scale in materials costs, especially if a manufacturer is paying more in total for the various components together than it would for a complete outsourced system. It has to be assumed that a system supplier will get much better discounts on its large purchases of individual components.

3. Productivity: Manufacturers often lag well behind suppliers in productivity, quite apart from economies of scale. In order to identify total productivity—beyond manufacturing—in a facility where up to 50 percent of staff work in indirect functions, a benchmark needs to be developed that includes indirect labor. This will include such general ratios as the total number of hours (direct and indirect) per product, or—as an indicator of how lean a manufacturing organization is—the number of productive hours divided by the total number of employees at the facility.

Here, too, suppliers frequently have a 20 to 30 percent advantage. The reason is simple: supplier companies, steeped in organizational transparency, an owner-based culture, and entrepreneurship are often working with much more efficient structures and are far more productive than larger companies.

However, a company should not come to a hasty conclusion based on pure productivity disadvantages that cannot be attributed to factor cost or scale disadvantages. Ensuring adequate productivity is a management task that has to be addressed by other means than "eliminating" more and more value-added stages. But a company should also beware of overautomation ("If employees are expensive and unproductive, we will just have to do without them in future"). Such an approach has been known to lead to ruinous investment decisions with, at best, marginal productivity improvements in return.

4. Design-to-cost potential: Factor costs, scale effects, and productivity differentials should not be the only—and invariable—parameters in the outsourcing calculation. It is just as important to make careful estimates of the potential for further cost optimization. Logistics costs are a fruitful source. Not only does a manufacturer need to have low materials inventories, but also total warehousing, transportation, and setup costs need to be minimized for both manufacturer and supplier.

But perhaps the greatest improvement potential typically lies in design-to-cost. As a rule, improvements here are available only to the organization with the most experience in systems optimization and the best knowledge of the manufacturing processes involved. That may be the manufacturer. However, for important subsystems in particular, it is often the supplier. For example, the amount of expensive platinum needed for an automotive catalytic converter could be considerably reduced because a supplier's experience in flow optimization was applied at an early stage in the development process.

Design-to-cost potential is particularly high in cases where a supplier can tailor the design to fit its own manufacturing conditions better. One machinery manufacturer, for example, had always insisted on the use of a forging in one subsystem. However, its supplier was able to meet the same requirements with a sheet metal part that it could also produce much more cheaply with its existing plant, thus reducing costs considerably for both parties.

Close coordination and exchanges of experience between manufacturer and supplier often bring to light unexpected improvement opportunities. One German manufacturer sent a standard part to Japan for redesign and a comparative quotation. Its initial expectations were confirmed: the Japanese developer and producer could deliver about 30 percent cheaper. The company's surprise, when it tried again, with a more complex part, was all the greater. The Japanese supplier was some 18 percent more expensive than the German manufacturer, despite the redesign.

However, it would still have been wrong not to outsource—as was revealed by a more detailed analysis of the cost differences. Integrating the extremely complex part into the Japanese supplier's manufacturing process did cause major problems, made all the more explicit by the supplier's better cost accounting system, which showed the full cost of complexity. At the German customer company, by contrast, the simple parts were subsidizing the complex ones. Once the complexity costs had been properly allocated, the Japanese offer was still more cost-effective in the long term than in-house development.

A closer look at the Japanese supplier's redesign brought further rewards. On its own, the complex part offered practically no optimization opportunities, since it was interconnected with too many other parts and components. But optimization of the total system—redesign and new development of all the components by the Japanese supplier—revealed the full cost-reduction potential.

In both these examples, design-to-cost potential could only be exploited through increased subcontracting. But outsourcing isolated parts of production can also have a detrimental effect. One heavy engineering company decided some 10 years ago to reduce its vertical integration substantially and stop making parts completely. Since demand fluctuated considerably, it was assumed that converting fixed costs to variable would make the company more competitive.

Although this concept looked good initially, the drastic cuts almost destroyed the company. Because the cuts were confined solely to machine design, the developers lost their understanding of manufacturing processes, and their product/process optimization deteriorated accordingly. At the same time, suppliers were not prepared to optimize their own manufacturing processes to fit the products, since they never knew when the next order or frame contract was coming, or whether their contracts would be renewed.

In such an atmosphere of uncertainty, it was impossible to optimize procedures and processes. The company did not—as might have been expected—fall too far behind technologically, and remained perfectly competitive in the decisive systems technologies. But on the cost side, things looked less rosy. The nature of the interface between development and production made discussion and coordination difficult. As a result, the opportunity costs of forgone design-to-cost approaches were extremely high, and the company's overall cost position was no longer competitive.

A decision on vertical integration on the basis of technological differentiation is valid only in conjunction with a detailed cost analysis. If manufacturing is to be kept in-house for reasons of differentiation, it is essential to make its total cost transparent and suitably competitive. If a particular part does not serve technological differentiation and no cost advantages can be gained from in-house development and production, the manufacturer should switch to a strict policy of outsourcing. Here, getting the right form of collaboration with the supplier is at least as important as getting the original decision right.

COLLABORATION WITH SUPPLIERS: PARTNERSHIP, NOT DOMINANCE

Unilateral actions will not take a manufacturer very far toward meeting the needs and exploiting the improvement potential revealed by the technology and cost analyses. Realizing both design-to-cost potential and cost advantages depends on achieving the best form of cooperation with the right suppliers. Continuing to operate according to traditional styles of behavior can jeopardize—or even reverse—the advantages.

Once again, the basic winning rule is simplicity. The interface with the supplier should be designed in such a way that a clear delineation of the systems boundary simplifies the operations of the two companies and, at the same time, opens up technical improvement potential. The successful companies also simplify things for themselves and their suppliers by consistently creating a basis of trust. When the interests of both parties coincide from the outset, energies can be applied more productively to shared improvements rather than to a host of checks and controls.

Systems Boundary

The right systems definition is *the* critical direction setter in the overall outsourcing process. Mistakes here cannot be made up for even if all the other conditions are more than fulfilled. The overriding criterion for the right systems definition is very simple: What system will allow the manufacturer to achieve technological differentiation and at the same time allow optimum exploitation of factor, scale, productivity, and design-to-cost potential? Two main questions are uppermost in practice: What interface should be chosen, and how large should the subcontracted system be?

Interface: There are three types of interface to be considered: families of parts, function modules, and assembly modules. In all three cases, a manufacturer will buy more from suppliers than it has done in the past, and the focus on one or a very few suppliers will allow a new form of collaboration. Which of the three interfaces to choose depends very much on the potential available.

+ If it decides on a family of parts, a manufacturer will stop buying, for example, its various actuators or hydraulic units from several sources, and buy them from one supplier as a family of parts. The greatest rationalization potential here lies in the fact that the supplier gains a complete overview of the manufacturer's needs and thus becomes a more competent partner. The supplier can help the manufacturer open up many more cost-reduction opportunities by standardizing its various control or drive units. Both manufacturer and supplier can then make considerable savings in specification and control.

  This approach will not normally reduce factor cost. Improvements will come primarily from economies of scale resulting from standardization, and to some extent from design-to-cost potential. From the manufacturer's point of view, it also means simplicity in supplier development, as it only has to develop one supplier instead of several.

+ At first sight, the most intelligent interface arrangement is to subcontract complete functional modules. Here, the interface between the supplier and the manufacturer is defined by the specification of functional requirements and installation conditions. Within this definition, the supplier can exploit every degree of freedom and, for example, shift various functions from one component to another. Management of the interface becomes problematic only if the functional module is "distributed" over the entire machine. There is then a risk that over-complex coordination processes will be needed, that design-to-cost potential will not be exploited, and/or that functional problems may arise.

  Subcontracting complete functional modules makes sense only when the supplier knows the systems architecture better than the manufacturer does, possibly because it supplies a large number of manufacturers.

+ The greatest cost advantages are normally achieved when complete assembly modules—which should ideally also be functional modules—are outsourced. The advantage of this unit is that the manufacturer has to handle it only once more, for final assembly. A high percentage of the assembly value added is shifted to the supplier—with corresponding improvements in personnel cost, economies of scale, and design-to-cost. Manufacturing and development can draw up specifications for assembly modules more easily than for families of parts and functional modules.

Almost every machinery manufacturer has experienced the advantages of buying complete assembly and functional modules. Many machinery makers have cut costs considerably by switching from the purchase of individual gear wheels to complete standard gears; and some suppliers of active spindle-bearing units, for example, now offer products far superior to most in-house alternatives.

The search for appropriate outsourcing modules should start with the largest possible packages of subassemblies, and proceed to a lower level of aggregation if no opportunities are found there. In extreme cases, it has actually proved wisest to buy entire product groups from external sources if the technology was extremely mature, if no further technological discontinuities were on the horizon, and if low volume prevented a manufacturer from gaining differentiation with the process technology. If subcontracting works successfully at the level of entire products or submodules, it also becomes more feasible to make the much-cited, largely residual fixed costs flexible after all.

Scope of supply: Once the interface has been defined, the question of the scope of supply arises. If it is too restricted, a supplier will have little room for optimization; if it is too broad, there is a risk that no supplier will have the resources to exploit the potential.

Basically a fairly generous scope makes sense when the system is largely separable—in other words, when the number of interfaces with other systems and subsystems is limited and the connecting parameters at the system interfaces can be precisely stipulated.

In deciding on the scope, it is important to have a clear understanding of a supplier's skills. When the scope is based mainly on logistical requirements, it can often put too much strain on the supplier. For example, if a supplier that only produces electronic parts needs to deliver both electronic and mechanical parts, it will quickly regard the mechanical ones as an added extra for whose costs it does not feel responsible—and those costs will soon start to rise.

A supplier can only achieve significantly better systems costs than a manufacturer if it develops and manufactures a large proportion of the components. In this way the supplier can optimize entire groups of components or aggregate individual functions, and thus make quantum leaps in cost or performance. Naturally, it is conceivable—particularly with mass production—that suppliers with different strengths will form a project-specific or multiproject alliance and make good package offers. The manufacturer needs to be careful here, however, since purchasing a system from two cooperating companies involves much greater effort from all participants than purchasing from only one supplier. Nevertheless, current trends favor collaborations of this kind, as can be observed in the automotive supply industry. This development will chiefly be successful if it brings manufacturers additional cost advantages.

Building Trust-Based Relationships

Optimizing the level of integration goes so deep into the internal structure of both manufacturer and supplier that a strong mutual dependency develops. This typically means that a manufacturer confines itself to a single supplier (single sourcing). The successful companies in our study are well down this track. In some 50 percent of cases they buy parts of a similar type from a single supplier. Only about 10 percent of the less successful competitors venture into such radical single sourcing (Exhibit 2-2).

While the less successful companies are wary of becoming dependent on a single supplier, the successful companies realized that this approach naturally makes the supplier much more dependent on the manufacturer, its customer. The volume of business from one customer increases, and obligations toward that customer are binding for much longer and include more significant responsibilities, such as setting annual rationalization targets for the life cycle of a specific machine.

In this context, the apparent truism that cooperation must be based on mutual trust cannot be taken seriously enough. But the necessary trust can be established only when the desired improvements bring advantages

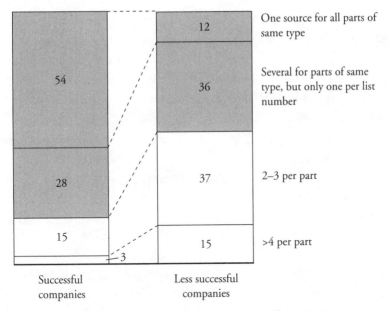

54	12	One source for all parts of same type
	36	Several for parts of same type, but only one per list number
28	37	2–3 per part
15	15	>4 per part
	3	

Successful companies | Less successful companies

Successful companies work with fewer suppliers/part/module.

Exhibit 2-2. Sources of Supply, 1989 (% of purchasing volume)

to both parties. An important sign of this is early commitment by both partners, so that their energies can be concentrated on further optimization of the substance and results of the collaboration rather than on staking claims and securing fall-back positions.

This, in turn, requires new procedures on the part of manufacturers. In particular, it means more demanding, less opportunistic definitions of what is required from suppliers; fast preselection of systems suppliers on the basis of a design competition; and a binding decision on the sole or main suppliers.

Requirements from suppliers: Traditionally, requirements from suppliers are often formulated on the basis of the pressures of the moment and functional self-interest. A manufacturer's design department may want to cooperate with the most competent developers in the early stages, long before purchasing is involved. Often, the supplier preferred by the designer is not at all attractive from a cost point of view. Consequently, purchasing normally insists that other—cheaper—suppliers are taken on, at least as second suppliers.

In many cases, the product is so firmly attached to the first supplier by this stage that no change is possible. Or purchasing may find a cheaper supplier that can at least cover partial deliveries. When this happens, the original supplier becomes concerned that a competitor will profit from its intellectual input; purchasing is dissatisfied at having to buy some of its materials from the "much-too-expensive" supplier; and the design department has difficulty motivating the most competent developer for the next project.

This vicious circle can only be broken by suppliers' meeting four key criteria:

+ Development know-how. Often, purchasing will suggest suppliers that may be able to produce at very low cost, but do not have the right design know-how. However, since the greatest potential frequently lies primarily in intelligent design-to-cost, such companies will not make the best partners. Even today, some companies still believe that they can solve this problem by doing the development themselves or subcontracting it to an engineering company, then giving the blueprint to a "garage company" for low-cost production.

  Generally speaking, however, savings from this approach exist only on paper, since de facto it prevents total product/process optimization. In many cases, the experiment ends in the supplier redrawing the engineering company's blueprints to turn them into production documents. To avoid such inefficiency, most suppliers, with the exception of a very few commodity makers, must have development know-how.

+ Manufacturing know-how and appropriate cost structure. It is clearly important for a supplier to have the know-how to achieve the desired technological level and planned volumes. But it is even more important to know, even before inviting entries for the design competition, whether a supplier can actually meet requirements in terms of its structural costs, logistics systems (on-time delivery), and quality standards.

+ Stability of the supplier as a business partner. Since a company is interested in selecting a single-source supplier, financially unsound companies with poor profitability and with no highly capitalized parent to bear liability should be excluded.

+ Loyalty. This criterion is certainly fulfilled in most cases. However, caution is needed, particularly when the supplier has close equity links with a major manufacturing competitor, or if the supplier feels that the manufacturer is not a particularly attractive customer.

Design competition: Suppliers that meet these criteria should be given the opportunity to enter a design competition based on clearly defined functional performance and cost goals.

Each of the goals must be realistic, yet ambitious enough to make thinking solely in terms of traditional systems architectures and production concepts inadequate. Suppliers should be expected to follow new tracks as well, and to submit proposals based on changed business conditions (for example, specification or complexity). It is important to reduce the possible suppliers to a manageable, but still sufficiently large, number— preferably three to five—after the competition, since the company will have to discuss the systems concept with the contenders in detail.

The preselection process should not go on too long. The best approach is to do it in overlapping stages, keeping the time for each system down to three to four months. The result will be a choice of suppliers based on several design offers, containing binding agreements on prices for the entire life of the product, including a clear understanding on the part of the supplier to rationalize further during ongoing series production.

Single sourcing: Choosing a single source and introducing intensive, trust-based collaboration can normally lead to cost savings of 30 to 40 percent; playing off several suppliers against one another brings single-figure improvements at best, and those are rarely sustainable. Moreover, emergencies—"Supplier threatened with bankruptcy"—can be largely avoided by following the selection process described.

Trust has to be earned. That means that a manufacturer should vet its partners for collaboration very carefully. Properly exercised, the new

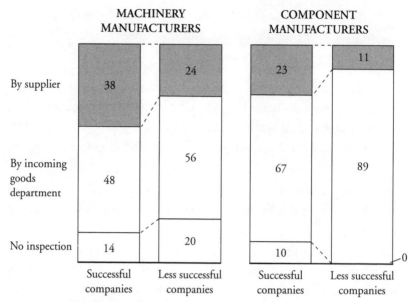

Successful companies have more sourced parts inspected by the supplier.

Exhibit 2-3. Quality Control of Sourced Parts
(% of purchasing volume)

trust makes great demands on both sides; on the other hand, it makes day-to-day business much easier. A large proportion of the productivity deficit in a manufacturer's indirect functions can be attributed to the need to check up on suppliers. From design, purchasing, and logistics through quality assurance, an enormous number of man-hours are often required, resulting in increased hidden costs for the manufacturer. The successful machinery and component manufacturers in our survey, by contrast, sometimes had quality control done by the supplier (Exhibit 2-3).

NEW MODES OF BEHAVIOR: PRACTICE MAKES PERFECT

Although the general vision of the new type of cooperation between manufacturer and supplier is often shared by top management on both sides, the day-to-day behavior of employees at all levels is often the main obstacle to overcome.

Seven out of ten decisions on vertical integration by successful German

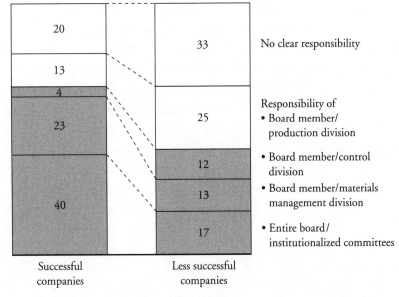

20	33
13	No clear responsibility
4	
23	25
	Responsibility of
	• Board member/ production division
40	12 • Board member/control division
	13 • Board member/materials management division
	17 • Entire board/ institutionalized committees

Successful companies   Less successful companies

In successful companies, cross-functional decision makers normally take make-or-buy decisions,

Exhibit 2-4. Responsibility for Strategic Vertical Integration Decisions (% of companies analyzed)

machinery and component manufacturing companies are made by "neutral," cross-functional decision makers. The rate for the less successful companies is only four out of ten; under these circumstances, the decision is normally made in production (Exhibit 2-4).

This issue touches on an important condition for optimizing vertical integration: skills and new styles of behavior throughout the organization, at both the manufacturer and the supplier. Among the successful companies, this change in behavior is championed by top management, and disseminated throughout the organization by a competent project leader. In implementation, the law of simplicity applies once again. Instead of being issued comprehensive and complicated general instructions, managers and staff at both companies have the opportunity to try out the unfamiliar, new-style objectives and approaches in real projects.

If short-term implementability encounters skepticism ("We can't change anything in the current machine design"), the pilot project should be handled as on-the-job training and be given a longer-term time horizon—for example, up to the changeover to a completely new machine concept. Often, it is possible to integrate quite a few of the new ideas for the next model into ongoing production. Besides the advantage of reducing costs even before the new model goes into production, step-by-step introduction also reduces risks during the changeover. If the company's change readiness is high and management is strong, such a change can usually be accomplished with a short time horizon.

A program of this kind is a powerful signal, making the extent of and the need for the changes clear to staff at both manufacturer and supplier. Once change readiness has been triggered, the change processes have to be vigorously implemented in the individual functions. This will work only if managers are willing and able to lead the movement, and if the company practices targeted job rotation between functions—chiefly between purchasing and development, but also manufacturing. This is because the necessary changes are often of an almost revolutionary nature. Let us illustrate.

Development/Design

There was a time when suppliers were often not involved until after the overall concept was fixed—after systems interfaces had already been implicitly determined and specifications more or less defined. In the new style of cooperation, by contrast, the development function has to define the most important systems, and thus the appropriate level of integration, in agreement with other functions at the outset.

This approach is very much in the interest of the development department, even if it means having to fix the systems architecture much earlier than it used to. (In principle, this change would be needed even if suppliers were not getting more involved, but it is not current practice in most development and design departments.) What is not so much to the developers' taste is the fact that they can no longer call in a supplier of their choice casually at short notice, but have to obtain the agreement of a cross-functional group.

For the development function, such change is quite fundamental. It means having to relinquish the detailed design of subcontracted systems.

Logically, it should also mean buying prototype parts from the series supplier and having the supplier perform the component tests. Only in this way can a manufacturer optimize its total costs by introducing "lean management"; only in this way will a supplier realize from the outset that it alone has full responsibility, and can no longer rely on being second-guessed by the manufacturer.

Purchasing

In the past, purchasing's main activity was often the annual negotiation, in which the department tried to keep prices constant despite inflation. By contrast, the purchasers of the future will be judged by whether they can build up detailed know-how on their suppliers' cost structures and performance capabilities, and use it when negotiating long-term contracts. Such know-how will also make it possible to involve superior suppliers in the preselection stage. Although today's purchasing departments are usually aware of the traditional suppliers, often they have not heard of world-class international players.

This knowledge is also useful in contract negotiations, since it helps in understanding a supplier's scope of action. Manufacturers that know a supplier's costs and still leave it a profit margin are cleverer in the long run than those that try to squeeze out every last advantage. Partnership is possible only when it is based on fairness.

Management Control

At first sight, the control function might be expected to change least in the new order. Often, however, it will have a particularly hard struggle, since it has to discard the long-prevailing marginal-cost approach. Now it has to determine the full cost of components and subsystems under different scenarios early in development, and estimate how far fixed costs can be cut if the level of integration is reduced. To achieve truly sustainable cost cuts, it must aim for proportional reductions—higher ones would be even better—in the indirect functions and drive through the corresponding change processes.

In addition, control has to perform detailed cash-flow calculations to enable management to compare offers from different suppliers with the cost of in-house manufacture.

Production

By their very nature, most decisions on reducing vertical integration will entail far-reaching changes in production. It is here that a sustainable concept must be developed first, building on the corporate goal of technological differentiation.

A company must decide which of the modules or systems that are not essential for technological differentiation can still be "offered" competitively by in-house production. Their competitiveness must be measurable against the criteria of factor cost, economies of scale, productivity, and design-to-cost. By these benchmarks, in-house production will often measure up to that of suppliers only if the divisions concerned are spun off as profit centers, where possible with their own design/development departments—becoming, in a sense, suppliers themselves. These units should then concentrate more on design-to-cost potential, and, in the medium to long term, on achieving structural cost advantages as well— in particular, lower factor costs.

Moreover, with vertical integration reduced, production not only has to cut direct costs, but also adapt its overhead to match. Ideally, it should be possible to reduce the overhead more than proportionately. In our experience, facility size is no advantage when it comes to infrastructure costs; rather, the relative "administrative effort" increases with size. The only justification for large production facilities is economies of scale—for process technologies that are only cost-effective above a certain level of production. Apart from that, "small is efficient" is practically a law of nature. Overhead costs should therefore drop by a disproportionately greater amount as vertical integration is reduced. But that is possible only if the infrastructure and manufacturing hierarchies are challenged aggressively and changed accordingly.

Organizational inertia can only be overcome with precise, tough targets, derived from best-practice benchmarks and extrapolations from a company's current position. This is the only way to challenge and, if necessary, change entire hierarchical levels or supporting functions such as internal transport and maintenance. Restructuring logistics is a simpler and more straightforward adjustment than changing manufacturing and assembly, although here, too, in-house processes such as receipt of goods or transportation should be thoroughly examined.

Quality Assurance

For quality assurance, the new mode of collaboration with suppliers is a good opportunity to formulate the changes that need to be made in any case. Quality aspects should be taken into account as early as the initial stage of the supplier selection process, and a detailed quality audit should be carried out for the final selection. Moreover, quality control should specify the overriding quality targets for components and systems/modules even in the early phase of development.

As a result, quality assurance will actually have less work to do in the systems production phase. Even today, successful companies are relying more on a supplier's outgoing inspections and reducing their own checks on incoming goods. But this level of trust in suppliers is still fairly low: just under 40 percent for the successful machinery makers and a little more than 20 percent for the successful component manufacturers. That, too, indicates a need for action on optimizing vertical integration and building trust-based cooperation with suppliers.

✦ ✦ ✦

SUCCESSFUL MACHINERY and component manufacturers can reduce their total cost for a subsystem by up to 40 percent by optimizing their level of vertical integration. This optimization has to cover the entire value-added chain, including the structures and processes of suppliers. This is the only way to exploit the most important improvement potentials: outsourcing of entire systems, design-to-cost to meet the needs of both partners, and reliance on a small number of key suppliers.

- ✦ Strategic concentration by a manufacturer leaves only those parts and systems to in-house production that allow competitive technological differentiation at favorable cost. Outsourcing is focused on a far smaller number of suppliers—half to one-third of the previous number, with a clear preference for single sourcing and joint efforts to improve efficiency in the total process.

+ Interfaces are greatly simplified and reduced. Clear systems boundaries ensure security for both manufacturer and supplier, while leaving considerable scope for optimization, particularly for design-to-cost by suppliers. A manufacturer can cut the number of interfaces by subcontracting entire subsystems to one supplier rather than assembling components from various suppliers itself.

+ Changed procedures promote the building of trust between manufacturer and supplier. A manufacturer sees itself as a partner rather than as an overseer, and a supplier has accordingly more responsibility for development, prototype parts, component tests, and quality assurance at series production.

Depending on the company, and, above all, on the strength of its management, the change process will take from two to five years. The primary limiting factor is skills. With the current move toward retrenchment of older and often more highly skilled employees, this could indeed become severely limiting—even critical. Changes in behavior are essential at both manufacturer and supplier. The deciding factor is a committed management team with a strong will to change.

3
DEVELOPMENT

✦ ✦ ✦ ✦ ✦ ✦ ✦ ✦ ✦ ✦ ✦

Minimizing Risk with a Strong Upstream
Focus and an Integrated Approach

*M*OST manufacturers are aware that short product-development ment cycles have rich payoffs: they lead to marketable products faster, better, cheaper. What is also clear is that, since between 50 and 75 percent of a product's costs are typically determined at the development stages, they can have an inordinately high impact on a company's competitive position. What is less clear is the roadmap for achieving short development cycles and reducing costs through intelligent development.

Companies take a number of different routes. One U.S. electronics manufacturer had two parallel teams develop a product concept, one taking the company's usual approach, the other working on a low-cost alternative. The result: a better-performing product, with 10 percent lower manufacturing costs because it was easier to make. The annual savings on manufacturing alone totalled $7 million.

Other companies pour significant resources into product development and production engineering training. Ford, for example, trained 10,000 employees in design-to-cost. The result: improved—and simplified— designs that reportedly save the company $1.2 billion per year, or $700 per vehicle, which can be passed on to customers. According to some estimates, Ford's manufacturing productivity—measured in assembly hours per unit—is almost on a par with that of the best Japanese companies.

Improved product development leads not only to significant cost savings but also to faster product introduction and higher sales growth. A similar survey of U.S. component manufacturers found that successful companies are growing their sales at 3 to 4 percent annually—and at 15 to 20 percent in new-product offerings—compared to their less successful counterparts, which are losing sales overall by 3 to 4 percent annually, with new-product offerings accounting for a mere 2 percent increase. This difference is in no small measure due to better and more focused funding and more successful new-product development efforts. Moreover, the successful U.S. companies believe their superior products—created through superior development—command a price premium of some 5 percent, which cannot be achieved by the less successful competitors.

Performance leaps of this kind are achieved by making radical changes in thinking, and by breaking with traditional approaches in development work—moves that less successful companies find very hard to cope with. The process of integrated product development calls for combining know-how and competence across functional and hierarchical boundaries. In product design in particular, such concentrated application of competence can achieve quantum leap improvements by easy-to-manufacture designs with relatively little effort. Comparable progress from operational improvements in production, however, can only be achieved through a multitude of painstaking, small individual measures.

Achieving this cultural change successfully will bring additional improvement opportunities, far beyond mere cost savings in development. Chief among them are:

Strategic coupling: Integrated product development couples development strategy with corporate strategy. This is achieved through integrated product planning and development teams, which include representatives from all relevant functions and divisions, contributing experience, ideas, and judgment as equal partners and developing solutions together. Only with such a broad overview is it possible to implement the necessary long-term thinking in product design over several product generations.

Lower manufacturing cost and shorter development times and better quality: The cost savings from integrated product development are not necessarily obtained at the expense of lower quality or longer development

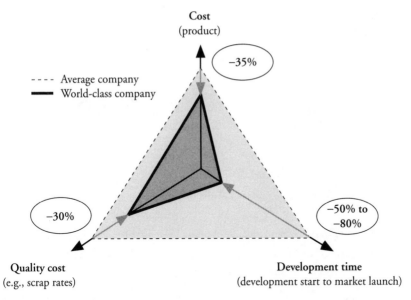

Cost
(product)

−35%

− − − − Average company
━━ World-class company

−30%

−50% to
−80%

Quality cost
(e.g., scrap rates)

Development time
(development start to market launch)

Successful companies do not achieve short development times at the expense of cost and quality.

Exhibit 3-1. Example: Machinery Manufacture

times (Exhibit 3-1). For example, successful companies in machinery and component manufacturing in Germany typically have a 35 percent manufacturing cost advantage over less successful performers; no less than one-third of this advantage is derived from design-to-cost. Product design has as much of an impact on cost-driving complexity in manufacturing, and is also responsible for locking in a large proportion of logistics costs (such as spare parts and spare parts supply), often over several decades.

Integrated product development is all this and fast, too. Consensus building in the team at the concept or other early development phases may be relatively time-consuming. But that is more than made up for by the smooth, disciplined execution of downstream development. Few changes occur downstream, so that time and cost are saved on complex, late hardware modifications. At less successful companies, even the actual concept phase suffers from above-average delays due to a plethora of modifications and points requiring clarification. As a result, successful machinery companies in Germany need half the time for the total development process (Exhibit 3-2).

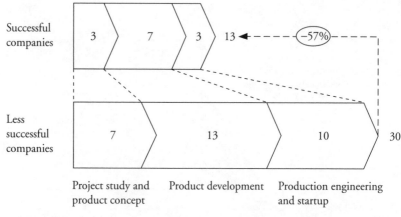

Successful companies	3	7	3	13 ◀ – – – – (–57%) – – – –

Less successful companies	7	13	10	30

Project study and product concept   Product development   Production engineering and startup

Successful machinery manufacturers have much shorter development times.
Exhibit 3-2. Manufacturers of Comparable Product Groups (development time in months)

It is in development time that we see one of the most significant differences between German and U.S. companies. The German companies take on average only half the time of their U.S. counterparts. In Germany, despite the sample being slightly skewed toward more complex machinery products versus the simple components manufactured by the U.S. sample companies, average development time is just over two years. In the United States, the successful companies take about 40 months and the less successful take close to a surprisingly long 50 months.

The most striking time gains in Germany are accomplished in the pre-phase with project study and concept development. Here, while the U.S. companies take 12 to 20 months—because they make many concept changes and miss clear deadlines—in Germany, the pre-phase is finished within about 5 months. In the main development phase there are no striking differences, both about 15 months. But again, the less successful German and all U.S. companies lose time in the production preparation and ramp-up phase (5 to 7 months versus 10 to 15 months).

Quality and low costs are not mutually exclusive. In the manufacture of comparable diagnostic equipment, for example, German company A was about average on manufacturing cost and quality, while its Japanese competitor B had 30 percent lower costs and still scored 30 percentage points more on the quality index. The main reason for company B's superior position was that it used modular designs with proven subsystems. This not only allowed for a higher share of perfect products after assembly, but also led to fewer faults in operation, which were also simpler to repair.

The successful companies' simple creed is to "design quality in" to a product, rather than "inspecting it in" or having it "repaired in" by sales and service. This is demonstrated in diagnostic equipment, machine tools, domestic appliances, and automobiles alike. The scale of the potential advantages varies by industry. In mechanically based industries, for example, the best companies outstrip their less successful competitors on average by 35 percent on cost, 30 percent on quality (measured by scrap rates or the cost of quality), and as much as 50 to 80 percent on throughput times.

In electronics, the successful companies' lead is even greater. Cost differences of 60 to 70 percent are not unusual. On the quality side, the less successful manufacturers often have as much as 10 times more soldering faults per board, and their throughput times are twice as long.

Naturally, these yawning gaps do not arise because of differences in product development alone; they also derive from different operational layouts and, to a lesser extent, from differences in factor costs. In almost every case, however, one-third to two-thirds of the gap can be closed by changing only product development.

And integrated product development does not necessarily generate particularly high development costs. For example, the successful machinery and component manufacturers in Germany spend much less on development, at 4.4 percent of sales, than the less successful players with approximately 6 to 8 percent. Their focused product range, however, makes this expenditure go much further per product: DM6.5 million per year compared to DM4.7 million per year at less successful competitors.

Motivation: Because of their involvement in multifunctional teams, employees get far more learning and development opportunities out of integrated product development than out of the traditional development approach. These are derived not only from increased responsibility and decision-making freedom, but also from the competitive advantage of motivation—a factor still frequently underestimated because it is hard to measure. Its concrete impact may possibly be deduced from experience in the manufacturing functions, where a direct correlation has been proved between worker motivation and absenteeism. A gain (or loss) in the development staff's commitment will surely be at least equally important.

The world standard for the type of efficient product development discussed here is today generally being set by Japan. So much so that Japanese superiority in labor productivity, time to market, and development cost is practically regarded as a law of nature. Yet it is a dangerous false assumption because it engenders paralysis. Using integrated product development properly, Western management should be able to turn the traditional Western strengths of individualism and creativity into competitive advantages. And there is no reason why existing operational differences should not be levelled out, apart, perhaps, from the factor cost differences, which, in any case, play only a minor role.

Is there any reason, for example, why European—or American— marketing and sales experts, working jointly with product developers, shouldn't be able to identify attractive segments and develop products for them? Is there any reason why they shouldn't be able to strip down superfluous product features and specifications? Is there any reason why they can't get their engineers (who are certainly no less capable than their Japanese counterparts) together with their opposite numbers in manufacturing or at suppliers, to arrive at an optimized product design which can be produced cost-efficiently?

In view of our traditionally shorter decision-making processes, our concept and upstream development phases, for instance, could actually be much shorter than in comparable Japanese companies. And downstream development has a good chance of catching up in speed and efficiency. The key obstacles, which should be taken very seriously, are a deeply rooted departmental and functional parochialism, a tendency to cling to incrementalism, and little inclination to make radical changes.

Integrated product development demands partner-like interaction both internally and externally. Such an approach calls for: uncompromising concentration on (in particular, latent) customer wishes, clarification of technology, and realistic planning upstream to minimize downstream risks; strategic involvement of suppliers across the entire development pro-

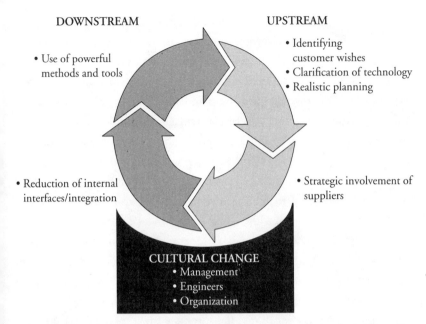

DOWNSTREAM

UPSTREAM

• Use of powerful
methods and tools

• Identifying
customer wishes
• Clarification of technology
• Realistic planning

• Reduction of internal
interfaces/integration

• Strategic involvement of
suppliers

CULTURAL CHANGE
• Management
• Engineers
• Organization

Integrated product development demands partner-like interaction both internally and externally.

Exhibit 3-3. Winning Activities in Development Process

cess; rigorous reduction of internal interfaces and increased integration; and finally, simple, effective, and powerful methods and tools to support the quantum leap in performance (Exhibit 3-3).

UPSTREAM DEVELOPMENT: THE ROLE OF THE "PLANNING INTELLIGENCE"

A new car, developed at a cost of DM2 to DM3 billion, lacks a through-loading facility for inserting skis or golf clubs from the trunk. Or a new machine tool cuts faster than ever before, but is so temperamental that down times for repair and maintenance destroy the benefits, since they ultimately lead to higher manufacturing costs. These examples are typical of innumerable cases where the results of expensive development projects have been disappointing because market requirements were either unknown, or were not taken sufficiently into account.

Often only a very small number of customer wishes, translated into product features, are responsible for a product's success on the market. For example, does anyone know about and use all the hundred or more functions of his or her office telephone system? How many of them were relevant to the buying decision? If a manufacturer piles every possible bell and whistle onto a product, out of ignorance or uncertainty as to the market's real needs, the end result is unlikely to be competitive, however well it performs. It will be too expensive and possibly too complicated as well.

Because of the complexity generated, such manufacturers generally forgo the opportunity to hit the market quickly with a product that is really innovative in a few, truly relevant performance features, and to skim higher margins with a temporarily unique selling proposition. Moreover, it is only natural that the higher the number of product features is, the greater will be the risk in the overall development process. In our experience, doubling the complexity does not lead to double the risk. Because of the interfaces between individual product functions and the need to integrate—if only into a single mechanical housing or software package—risk often increases exponentially, even to the extent of becoming uncontrollable.

Customer-specific modifications are just as bad if they are carried out retrospectively for strategically unimportant customers. The survey results in Germany showed that while such modifications do increase sales, they also place a strain on return and liquidity. At component manufacturers, for example, making changes is relatively easy, but the overall profit impact is still negative. The problem is much worse in machinery manufacture, where customer-specific adaptations are comparatively expensive, contribute only little to sales growth, and reduce return on sales considerably.

Such information, however, is not commonly known among companies, which confuse the issue with questions of being responsive to customer wishes. So the successful companies in both Germany and the United States make more customer-specific adaptations for really important customers, while they avoid becoming overcomplex by reacting to every adaptation wish of every minor customer. Overall levels of customer-specific adaptation seem to be considerably higher in Germany than in the United States, which may help explain Germany's high levels of development spending and overcomplexity.

Understanding these causes and effects in as much detail as possible is a top-priority development task. That was demonstrated by the manufacturer of a diagnostic instrument, whose manufacturing costs were 41 percent higher than those of its main competitor. About 22 percentage points of these additional costs could be traced back to design differences, which design-to-cost measures could help eliminate; a further 8 percentage points were due to performance features that commanded a premium in the market. But a full 11 percentage points of the cost disadvantage were attributable to features the customer was not willing to pay extra for.

The best companies have detailed knowledge of these mechanisms for all their products. They know they have to consider the consequences as early as upstream development. It is far easier to achieve targeted orientation to customer wishes in the concept phase than it is, for example, to eliminate design-related cost disadvantages in the final downstream phases, when production equipment is already planned and set.

For upstream development to perform this role, it has to become the "planning intelligence" of the company, and be given corresponding importance. Clear decisions on the direction of development, derived from listening to customers, must be taken upstream and then implemented in a disciplined manner downstream. The best companies set clear priorities accordingly:

+ There is greater focus on upstream activities.

+ Developers gain an understanding of customer value from personal observation.

+ The use of certain technologies is clarified at the outset from a long-term perspective.

+ In development tactics, a "small-steps" approach continuously explores room for improvement.

+ Sound, analytically based development planning makes risk and profitability more or less calculable.

In all these actions, it is clear that only integration of all the knowledge present in the company will produce the desired result. Upstream development that takes place in an ivory tower, or is coupled unilaterally with the development function, will not achieve such integration.

Greater Focus on Upstream Activity

The successful German machinery and component manufacturers spend about 16 percent of their total development budget upstream, a higher share than their less successful competitors, at 12 percent. It is worth the effort, since it makes downstream development less risky, simpler, and more manageable.

Already at the upstream stage, information from competitor and market observation needs to be evaluated as input for new product concepts. Most companies usually have a wealth of data on competitors, from observation at trade fairs or from employees who previously worked for competitors. In most cases, however, such data are not properly analyzed or used to best effect. If consideration of these data is included in the move to increase the focus on upstream development, possibly by an integrated team set up for the purpose, they are an invaluable source of information for every department in the company, from which ideas for new technology concepts or products can be directly derived.

By the time upstream development is completed, three out of four of the successful machinery and component manufacturers in Germany have produced a project study with a list of specifications; only one in four of the less successful companies do that. But the successful companies do not make the mistake of dictating all the performance features at the outset; many—the minor ones—will be changed later. Only those features with long development lead times are finalized, and they stay finalized—in keeping with the motto: As late as possible, as early as necessary. As a result, while the successful manufacturers need an average of only six pages for their specifications, the poorer players need twenty.

Developers to the (Customer) Front

If a developer can see for herself a customer struggling with the product, it tells her more than if she hears about it at fifth hand from service, marketing, and sales. Not only do customers have good ideas, developers are more likely to identify new segments—which might provide an opportunity to establish even a short-lived unique market position—if they have direct customer contact. A developer needs to understand customer value better than the customer does. Only then can she transform latent customer wishes into creative technical solutions.

The simplest way to identify customer value is through direct observation of (potential) customers in their everyday environment. Developers from an electronics company, for example, visited a large recording studio and saw that the old analog audiomixers had major utilization problems. Perhaps a philharmonic orchestra had been recording classical music under its star conductor during the day, and the sound engineer had carefully set the desired tone, not only to his own liking but also to that of the orchestra and the conductor. That particular audiomixer could not be used again until the orchestra's next recording session, without undoing all that painstaking tuning effort. As a result, it was impossible, for example, to record rock music with the same audiomixer at night. Systems costing up to DM250,000 could be used for only one shift.

A new product feature which could be produced easily with existing digital technology brought about a major improvement—one whose importance its developers would undoubtedly have underestimated had they never been to the studio. With the new feature, all the parameters can be stored digitally at the end of a session, and each individual sound engineer can save his own preferences on disk. As a result, audiomixers and studio equipment can be reset in a very short time. This new, higher utilization—including a two-shift operation—enabled the manufacturer to sell the new digital audiomixer at a much higher price, while delivering enhanced economic value to the customer.

This consistent orientation to decisive customer value can only be achieved by developers. At one Japanese automotive manufacturer, for example, it is the norm for developers of models for the U.S. market to spend several weeks living in American households. Product design is optimized through detailed observation—of such details as how trunks are loaded in parking lots at Disneyland or at large supermarkets. Setting up local design studios also helps match design, one of the most important car-buying criteria, to local taste.

Our long-term study of machine and component manufacturers in Germany confirmed that the successful companies are strongly customer focused in their search for ideas. In fact, discussions with customers proved to be the most important source of ideas. Lagging well behind that came observation of competitors, then monitoring patents and trade literature, and attending conferences. Like speeders on U.S. highways, the best companies look ahead with radar detectors, so to speak, rather than keeping their eye on the rear-view mirror. For the poorer players, on the other hand, forward-looking activities are much less important. They rely too often on me-too strategies and products, while their more successful competitors move into new customer or technology segments.

Clarifying Technologies

Before the start of downstream development, as many as possible of the technologies to be included in a new product should already have proved their functionality. In a new aircraft, for example, the wings, the cockpit, or parts of the avionics should already have flown in test planes or as substitute parts in existing aircraft. This tactic naturally presupposes that the new product has been planned with a healthy amount of modularity—another important task at the interface between nontype-specific and type-specific upstream development.

Relying on individually tested components and on functioning technologies prevents unpleasant shocks downstream and allows resources to be concentrated on the critical innovative elements. Going into downstream development with unclarified technologies will, by contrast, mean dissipating the company's resources to reach piecemeal solutions and producing results on time, if at all, only by going well over budget. The extra highly skilled resources required for such downstream fire fighting are often recruited from upstream, which reduces upstream effectiveness and sets off a vicious circle that threatens the success of the next product generation as well.

Apart from basic research experiments, pursuing parallel concepts upstream also serves to eliminate most risks and surprises downstream. Trying out even two or three alternative concepts upstream, including a very low-cost solution, is almost always better than economizing at this stage. Otherwise, the risk of having to change to a previously untried alternative downstream is too great.

The "Small-Step" Innovation Tactic

The tactic of small steps—practiced by half the successful German machinery and component manufacturers, but by only 18 percent of the less successful—has a number of advantages. It brings the company frequently to the customer's attention, with improvements that are relatively easy for the manufacturer to make, but provide significant customer value. Japanese machine-tool makers understand this well. For years now they have been introducing new features and innovations to their tools within the same "footprint," for which their customers have been willing to pay a premium because they went beyond the "zone of indifference." Also, small steps will not place too much strain on the development team, since it will be building on past achievements, and the very latest technological innovation can, on occasion, be kept for the next (rapidly approaching) generation. Furthermore, development procedures can generally be kept simpler. Japanese electronics companies excel at this approach—upgrading their telephone systems, recording equipment, and car stereos, for example, with small-step innovations that command a premium price from the customer.

Development in small steps also allows better exploration of the maximum possible innovation curve. Companies using this tactic will have the better product on the market in the long run. They increase their product value per R&D dollar faster than competitors that bet on big new developments. And they notice earlier when existing technologies are approaching their limit (Exhibit 3-4). Companies with long development cycles, on the other hand, always run the risk of continuing to look for a quantum leap

PRODUCT VALUE

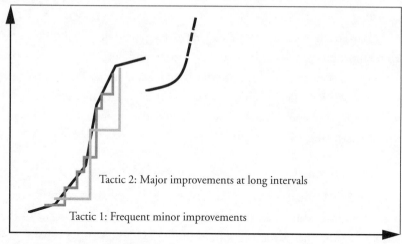

Tactic 2: Major improvements at long intervals

Tactic 1: Frequent minor improvements

CUMULATIVE R&D EFFORT

Frequent small improvements better exploit potential technical progress.
Exhibit 3-4. Tactics Along Technology S-Curves

when it is no longer either technologically possible or economically viable. This was the experience of the ship builders at the close of the sailing ship era. They did not realize that, after a certain point, they could not gain further speed by adding to the ship's length or increasing its sail area.

A prerequisite for success with the tactic of small, rapid steps is a thorough knowledge of the different life cycles of key product components. In the electronics industry, for example, the base technologies (such standards as VHS or CD) survive for at least five to seven years or even longer; mechanical modules (such as belt drives) have to be changed after about four years; and electronic modules (such as noise suppressors) have a life expectancy of two years at most.

A special form of small-step innovation is the game of "parents" and variants. If high, initial one-off investments are needed for product development, losses in the parent generation have to be compensated for with profitable variants. In the aircraft industry, for instance, there is virtually no parent type that could have made profits on its own, without variants. The highest contributions to profit come from variants that can use large parts of the past development work and that can be introduced in rapid succession. For this reason alone it makes sense in such industries to have upstream development design a whole product line, which can then be introduced in small development steps, rather than as a single product.

The rapid frequency of small technology steps calls for high flexibility in the product startup phase. This is achieved not with superexpensive, fully flexible production facilities, but by radically reducing setup times. Japanese car manufacturers, such as Honda, "practice" with new products on the old assembly lines before actually starting production. This also makes it possible to use old production lines and equipment to a large extent for the new products, saving considerable investment.

It is evident that the successful machinery and component makers in our German sample thoroughly understand all this. At these companies, the tactic of frequent, small innovations has a clear positive correlation with growth and return. It is all the more surprising that many of the companies do not see this approach as a particular strength. They tend to bundle their many minor value improvements as "releases"—precisely the development tactic that characterizes the less successful players. Only the coordination effort entailed by release bundles—and their frequent changes—stands in stark contradiction to simplicity. And the quantum leap approach accounts for part of the vulnerability of those manufacturers that make major improvements at long intervals.

The most successful winning tactic—in the two industries studied, at least—appears to be: every time the benefit of an innovative feature crosses the customer's perception threshold, offer a product with this feature. Micro-improvements that are not immediately obvious and macro-changes that attempt giant strides seem to promise less success than a continuous stream of genuine improvements in individual features that have real customer value.

Development Planning with a Sense of Realism

Where costs are allocated honestly, some product developments will cost so much before they even reach the market that they may threaten the company's very existence. If the development cost of a new model amounts to almost half a company's equity, as in the automotive industry, or even more, as in aircraft manufacturing, a failure will severely endanger the company's health. The time and potential sales lost are even worse than the "wasted" development cost. Cost structures cannot be adjusted as fast as sales of a poorly developed product collapse. And lead times for developing an alternative are often unendurably long.

Companies scoring regular hits despite pressure from shrinking life cycles do so because they adopt an approach of thoroughly realistic development planning. They assess objectively and accurately the factors that influence product profitability, their own competitive position, and the risk of market launch.

Product profitability: Most of the many ways of influencing product profitability—such as investment, personnel cost, and materials cost—are well known, although almost no company systematically exploits their full potential. Other leverage points, such as facility location or changes in working hours, are often considered impossible to influence for fear of new complications. But perhaps the most important lever, simplicity—or overcomplexity—is not monitored by traditional management information systems and is therefore rarely consciously applied.

Achieving consistent success with product introductions does not call for fragmenting a company's energies by trying to fulfill every conceivable success factor perfectly, and all at the same time. The best companies adjust to the cost structure of their industry over the product life cycle. They know precisely where to achieve the greatest impact with the least effort, and thus have complete control over the "game of sensitivities."

In the automotive industry, for example, with its high unit volumes, reducing materials consumption and unit cost is the key to higher profitability. Here, management of variable costs is the deciding factor. In the aircraft, semiconductor, or telecommunications industries, return on investment is determined largely by up-front expenditure. In this case, reducing R&D costs or distributing them over several partners is the most important leverage point.

Finally, in consumer electronics, getting to the market early is usually the deciding factor; the later a product is launched, the less time remains for pioneering profits to be skimmed. The first player that brought to market a car radio with a digital frequency display in the 1980s, for example, won not only market share, but also price premiums of 10 to 15 percent. The additional cash flow from such premiums in the period when this company was the only source of supply was enough to recoup the entire development cost.

Competitive position: The successful companies only take the risk of introducing a new product if they are close to the world-class competitive standard in the decisive, most sensitive parameters. What could be easier than following what the world's best competitor has already achieved? Yet although they know better, many companies often fail to follow this obvious rule.

It is widely known in the aerospace industry, for example, that certain minimum numbers of a commuter aircraft have to be sold over the life cycle; or, in the automotive business, that short development times and competitive manufacturing costs are the ticket to profitable markets. Yet aircraft programs are still launched when the market potential indicates that new players will not sell enough units to make a profit. Or diagnostic equipment manufacturers will overspecify their products so much that they are beyond the means of the broad market segment of general practitioners, yet are never able to achieve profitable unit sales in the much smaller hospital segment.

When a company asks critical questions, measures its own activities by world standards, and has the courage to take decisions, even unpleasant ones, in good time, this all serves to simplify the development process and make it more effective and profitable. Similar realistic assessment of their competitive position can also be seen in the product parity analysis carried out at successful machinery and component manufacturing companies in Germany. Both development managers and general managers of successful companies put the share of their own products that are superior to competitive offerings at just over 50 percent (in terms of sales). In less successful companies, development managers put this measure at about 70 percent, while general managers estimate it at just under 40 percent.

Market launch risk: The risk in introducing new products comes primarily from uncertainty about market potential and costs. The successful companies monitor in detail and manage those levers with the greatest impact on product profitability. Development is not started until sufficient purchase options have been obtained to guarantee a minimum unit volume. Or they get their customers' engineers closely involved in development to ensure that product specifications are precisely met. If complexity is the lever with the greatest impact, small development teams are set up to analyze and increase the use of identical parts for each component, as was the case with a major U.S. engine manufacturer. Or the development components with the highest risk are identified by probability analyses, and carefully monitored and controlled by management.

Further very simple opportunities for limiting risk are available through two conservative but effective measures for reducing investment: sharing one-off costs, through cooperations, joint ventures, or government grants (known in the business as OPM: other people's money); or using amortized components or processes from earlier programs (known as SOS: same old stuff).

Another very simple and effective method of reducing risk, unfortunately all too seldom used, is early discontinuation of projects when it becomes clear that they have no prospect of success. One spectacular example of the fatal consequences of taking the simplest action too late is the Lockheed Tristar. The new aircraft, for which project planning started in 1969, was expected to reach break even at 300 units.

From the outset, the fact that the concept was identical in many ways to the parallel development of McDonnell-Douglas's DC 10 was a major concern. Four years later, Rolls-Royce was on the brink of bankruptcy after problems with the engine and Lockheed itself was surviving only with government support. That would have been the time to discontinue the project, at a loss of some $400 million and shut-down costs of some $300 million. Instead, the projections were cosmetically improved, and a new break-even volume of 500 units was assessed as feasible, even though the almost identical DC 10 was aiming at the same market segment.

When production finally ceased in 1982, Lockheed had sold only 244 aircraft. In 13 years total losses had swelled to about $2.5 billion, plus about $400 million for the belated shutdown. That heralded Lockheed's departure from civil aircraft construction. The simple solution, a bold early decision, might have prevented the escalation of costs.

EXTERNAL SUPPLY RELATIONSHIPS: STRATEGIC TASK SHARING

As in manufacturing, a high level of vertical integration in development is not good or bad in itself. Successful companies with efficient development tend not to buy much in the way of development services. Companies lacking such operational efficiency seek partners for the development of parts and components. The important thing is for a company to make the best use of both its own and its suppliers' strengths. In extreme cases, that can mean spinning off entire functions.

Decisions on in-house or external development have a considerable impact even beyond the development function. Management targets for development integration may affect the strategic orientation of the entire company. Make-or-buy decisions in development often anticipate the level of vertical integration in manufacturing, since a part developed outside will, in all probability, be lost to in-house manufacture as well.

Such decisions are therefore so important that they should not be left solely to those directly affected in the development department. But above all, management should ensure that the chosen configuration of development integration incorporates all the key elements. That entails building up a network of high-performance development suppliers, and establishing the necessary in-house arrangements for fostering efficient cooperation. As part of that effort, suppliers must be involved from the outset in integrated product development (Exhibit 3-5).

Streamlining the Supplier Structure

Limiting the number of suppliers reduces cost, but, above all, creates new opportunities for closer and more effective cooperation.

The successful machinery and component manufacturers in Germany spend 11 percent of their total development budget on external development. So, too, do their less successful competitors. The difference lies in

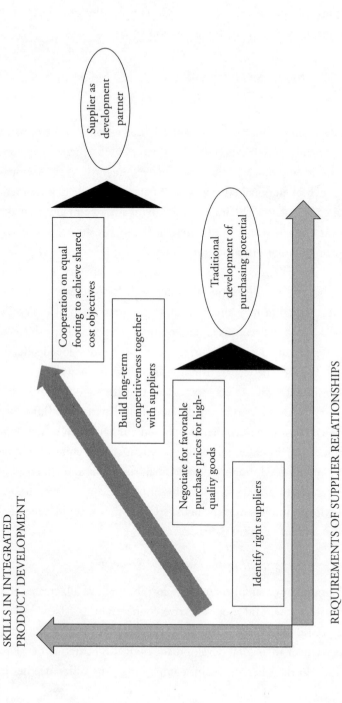

SKILLS IN INTEGRATED
PRODUCT DEVELOPMENT

Supplier as
development
partner

Cooperation on equal
footing to achieve shared
cost objectives

Build long-term
competitiveness together
with suppliers

Traditional
development of
purchasing potential

Negotiate for favorable
purchase prices for high-
quality goods

Identify right suppliers

REQUIREMENTS OF SUPPLIER RELATIONSHIPS

Integrated product development involves suppliers from the beginning.

Exhibit 3-5. Cooperation with Suppliers

the content of the development contracts. While the successful companies subcontract entire subassemblies, the less successful players tend to go outside for parts. This results in the development of a host of hard-to-manage interfaces with a large number of suppliers. This is a serious impediment to success, since it not only takes up valuable management time, but also means that only a small part of the significant design-to-cost potential can be realized.

There seems to be an important message here for U.S. companies. The degree of overall supplier integration is far higher in Germany than in the United States, where the successful companies are just beginning to pursue this improvement level.

In the long term, a company needs to set up a geographically favorable structure of development suppliers (close proximity clusters). Only those items for which full specifications can be drawn up—for example, electronic components with few interfaces such as telephone end-user equipment—can be successfully developed and built in remote, low-cost countries. In such cases, the imperative is not to give up at the first sign of quality problems. With a little patience and joint quality improvement programs, surprisingly simple and efficient relationships can often be built with low-cost suppliers.

Coupling Vertical Integration of Development and Manufacturing

If a functional subassembly is developed in-house, new production equipment is almost invariably installed to produce it. When a new model replaces an old one, development is under pressure to have the new component produced in-house again, and within the existing cost structures. This can lead to significant disadvantages and create a vicious circle.

No less dangerous than undifferentiated in-house development is the opposite extreme: choosing a supplier that offers temptingly fast development, but whose manufacturing costs are too high. To avoid committing to excessively expensive external manufacture in this situation, a company should break down the service. Development should be paid for separately, leaving room for negotiation with other suppliers on scale production, even if this freedom is used only in rare, exceptional cases. In the case of any part where a mold is involved, for example, a company should avoid contracting out development and production.

Joint Development

The successful companies are not only characterized by their very low number of suppliers. They also encourage those they do retain to grow into the role of emancipated development partners. These relationships begin at a very early stage, with joint elaboration of specifications so that the suppliers' entire know-how base can be used, and include regular coordination on development progress and checks on milestones.

Successful companies avoid the cardinal error of the less successful, which, for lack of resources or know-how, subcontract the development of entire systems—the strategically most important part. Although this approach may appear to solve a lot of problems, it also means that the company's know-how base will be lost, or may never be able to develop in the first place.

The winning formula, as successful companies know, is to subcontract not individual parts or the key task of systems integration, but complete subcomponents. At the same time, agreed-on progress control at certain milestones should be used to impose discipline on outside developers. This kind of close cooperation typically leads to even better adherence to schedules and specifications than working only in-house.

Strengthening In-House Sourcing Competence

The typical purchasing department is functionally separate from development, and is staffed with commercial personnel with no special technical know-how. However, since on average 50 percent of the cost of a finished product—that is, the materials cost—is determined in purchasing, it is particularly crucial for technology-based companies to ensure that purchasing and development work together closely and constructively.

A number of approaches can be taken to ensure that this happens. Especially effective techniques include job rotation of developers into purchasing and back, or joint purchasing by cross-functional project teams staffed with members from purchasing, development, and manufacturing.

DOWNSTREAM DEVELOPMENT: REDUCING INTERFACES

Because they focus more closely on upstream activities, the successful machinery manufacturing companies can succeed with leaner downstream functions. However, at the same time they ensure that these functions are better staffed and equipped. They go for quality rather than quantity. In Germany, total expenditure on new development by the successful companies as a percentage of sales is only half that of the less successful companies. However, in terms of expenditure per development employee per year, it is much higher, at DM205,000 compared to DM136,000.

By the time they start on downstream development, the successful companies have eliminated the most serious development risks. Upstream, they have gone to great lengths to identify customer wishes, have already translated them as far as possible into technical concepts, and have started sharing out tasks between in-house development and subcontractors. From now on, the issue is to turn the approved solutions systematically and efficiently into the finished product.

With this change in emphasis between upstream and downstream development, some aspects of the working environment will also change. Whereas upstream development is now given the greatest possible freedom to be creative and to cast its net widely in its search for ideas, and is allowed to make mistakes and fail, downstream development is expected to make uninterrupted progress and to adhere rigidly to schedules and budgets. At this stage, even the smallest error is one too many.

Another feature of upstream development work is retained downstream; that is, integration of know-how and skills from all relevant functions, departments, and levels. This integration actually tends to be more important downstream, since it is at this stage that decisions on expensive prototypes and test beds, and on the even more substantial investments in new tools and production facilities are taken.

Integration is fostered by appropriate organizational structures, supported by powerful technical aids and a redefinition of the development process. In addition, it is important to introduce development procedures that contribute to making staff really believe in integration, such as short feedback loops and new approaches to personnel development.

Integration by Organization

Not even as many as one in three of the successful machinery and component manufacturing companies in Germany still organize their development departments by technical function. Most are too well aware that the classical setup of a design engineering department (*Konstruktion*), followed by a test department is not the best way to achieve the short innovation cycles that are an imperative today. They realize that having too many interfaces means too much friction loss. As a result, 37 percent of the successful companies organize by product groups, and 17 percent by components such as mechanical/electronic parts. Of the less successful companies, only 25 percent and 8 percent, respectively, have such close-to-the-market structures.

Moreover, the successful companies make far more efficient use of their development staff, because they are expected to perform far fewer administrative and other noncore activities. In the less successful companies such nondevelopment activities take up as many as two-thirds of development working hours. In the successful companies, development engineers spend three-quarters of their time on product-related work. They achieve this despite having much less support—75 percent technical staff to 25 percent support staff—compared to the less successful companies, where this ratio is almost the reverse. What is the cause of such a striking difference?

The better all-round training and job rotation that the successful companies' engineers undergo fits them for multipurpose operation. One man will be able, for example, to design the layout for a printed circuit board, carry out its optimization and the mechanical engineering to fix it in its housing, and do the eventual associated production planning. With the integration of even some lower-valued tasks into the same job role, this approach outperforms functionally separated specialists in cost, time, and quality.

The same is true with setting up an experiment, which is better done by the researchers themselves, with only limited support from other staff, than delegated entirely to technicians. In that way they can be sure to get the right answers from the experiment and to know its limitations. And they have the added advantage of faster setup times. Researchers in successful companies are able to operate that way because they have better, more modern, and more expensive equipment, are better trained, and spend less time on their simpler administrative procedures.

In addition to organizing by product or component, two other structural forms can be used to support integrated, cross-functional development work. Depending on the individual characteristics of the product or industry, a team-oriented approach or a matrix structure may well be appropriate.

Product- or component-oriented organization is particularly appropriate where the interfaces between the individual products or components are relatively few and clearly defined. This is the case, for example, in machinery or component manufacture. In these cases, the commonalities between several product groups are rarely so strong that cross-technology structures can be used to exploit synergies. On the other hand, a product or component orientation helps increase sales opportunities, even at the development stage, because of the direct link to the market. However, in this type of organization, upstream and downstream development need to be clearly separated in order to maintain the differentiation, mentioned above, of approach in such areas as attitude to mistakes and failures.

Team-oriented organization is the best approach when speed is of the essence. An example of this approach is Honda's SED teams (sales, engineering, development). Honda Motor Company (sales), Honda Engineering Company (process engineering), and Honda R&D Company (development) all send their most experienced staff to these integrated product development teams. The appointed project managers choose their own subproject managers, for example for engine, drive train, or chassis development. The project manager and team also maintain contacts with suppliers.

Experience has shown, however, that there is one potential disadvantage to team organization. It can lead to a desire to optimize individual elements. An example might be wanting to have an engine cylinder head a few millimeters lower in the sports model of a car than in the corresponding sedan, so that the hood will be properly streamlined. This tendency to use fewer common parts between individual models, and thus to encourage cost-driving complexity, has to be rigorously kept in check.

Matrix organization, as practiced by Toyota, for example, attempts a compromise between product and team approaches. One axis of the matrix is formed by the Product Planning Office headed by a very high ranking general chief engineer, with chief engineers reporting to him as the product managers for the individual model series (e.g., the Corolla). On the other axis are the functional Design and Evaluation departments— for example, styling, body, engine, safety, emission, or noise. The advantage of this more complicated structure is the exchange of experience and exploitation of synergies between models. It means, for example, that insulating mats and other noise-absorbing components do not have to be reinvented by every project team. But the project chief engineer retains control and remains responsible for the success of his series throughout its life cycle.

This complex structure is, however, only worthwhile when it enables genuine synergies to be exploited. This typically happens only in rare cases and where market requirements are very similar. For its luxury model Lexus, for example, Toyota chose much more of a product-oriented organization, as IBM did for the PC. In both cases, closely meeting the individual requirements of different markets was considered more important than any presumed potential for synergy.

Whichever of these structures they choose, the successful companies support collaboration with effectively targeted use of technology. In Rank Xerox's design laboratory, for instance, the drafts of any of its specialists working at different CAD/CAM terminals can be displayed on two large monitors, which everyone can view. These terminals also have access to the company's worldwide engineering databases.

Short Feedback Loops

The main aim in downstream development is to perfect product functions and, at the same time, to simplify design engineering. In order to achieve this, the team elaborates in detail the product functions derived upstream from market requirements, optimizes them, then simplifies the design and draws up a process concept. At this stage there is a most important feedback process, during which engineering is further modified to meet process requirements (Exhibit 3-6).

The team will repeat this cycle several times, constantly improving product functions without allowing production processes to become too complex.

As these feedback loops become shorter, the results take effect faster and the learning effect becomes more sustainable. In teams composed of product developers, process developers/production planners, and production engineers, feedback processes are so short that genuine simultaneous engineering is possible. Feedback times are reduced from years or months to days or hours.

Since a similar kind of feedback loop will already have been applied in the upstream development phase, no major risks or surprises are really to be expected at the process concept stage.

New Approaches to People Development

Personnel development and career planning can play perhaps the most significant role in ensuring that the desired integration becomes reality. The successful companies typically reinforce tailor-made structures and new development procedures by new approaches in these areas, aimed at training and motivating development staff, development's key resource.

One of the advantages of Japanese companies is that, with development cycles two to three times faster, their development departments and development engineers have far more learning opportunities. While an engineer in the German automotive industry, entering employment at the age of 28 after finishing university, will only have developed one and a half cars by the time he reaches 40 (at a rate of eight years per development cycle), his Japanese contemporary, having started his career at about 24,

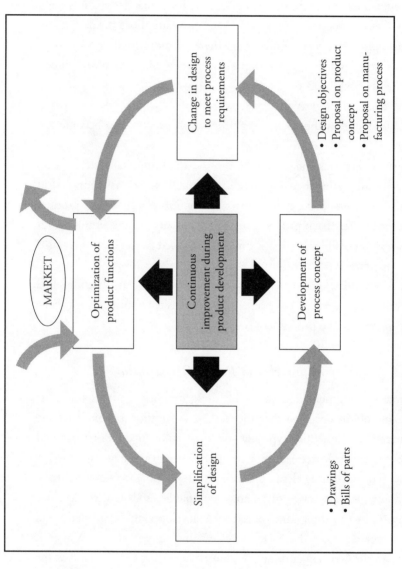

Continuous improvement and feedback into the development process optimize product and process.

Exhibit 3-6. Product and Process Optimization

will have four complete cars under his belt (at a rate of approximately four years per development) at age 40. For the United States, the comparable figures are 2.5 cars for an engineer starting his career at the age of 26— a rate of six years per cycle.

Some of the most effective approaches that seem second nature in Japan encounter cultural obstacles in Germany, and often in the United States, too. One such approach, for example, is to have a development engineer start his career on the production staff. This would be almost unthinkable in Germany. And yet it would be highly beneficial for all participants. An engineer with such experience would hardly be likely to infringe on basic production requirements in his subsequent designs. The division between "high-prestige" development and "second-class" production engineers would become less marked. And the approach would go a long way toward making up the enormous deficit of young, inventive production managers.

In Germany, ambitious technical experts who want to move up still typically have to opt for the management track, which means leaving their core technical expertise behind them. Long-term "expert" careers, which no longer depend on promotion through the managerial ranks, are only gradually being established in the successful companies.

Job rotation is a far more widespread practice. Indeed, this approach was one of the most striking differences between the successful and less successful companies in our long-term study. As many as 22 percent of the technical staff at the successful machinery and component manufacturers had switched in the past between production and engineering; in the less successful companies the figure was just 1 percent.

Besides the obvious benefits from increased know-how and broader perspectives, job rotation is also used to reduce the promotion backlog. A development engineer who passes through production, purchasing, sales, or even customer service can be given a new and interesting role every three to five years without being officially promoted each time. Several such lateral job changes may be the prelude to subsequent promotion— and they can also contribute to keeping overhead structures more manageable. They prevent the frustration caused by staying too long in one job, and alleviate the notorious tunnel vision of the blinkered functional specialist.

METHODS AND TOOLS:
NECESSARY BUT NOT SUFFICIENT

Getting simple, integrated product development right takes practice, and is typically accompanied by a radical change in corporate culture. The successful companies provide their engineers with ample opportunities to obtain the necessary practice. They challenge them constantly to determine how their product development will affect costs and customer value, and stimulate problem awareness and the will to change through competitor analyses (Exhibit 3-7). In all these activities, suitable methods and tools can help—not as a panacea, but to facilitate and support analysis and project work and to help in practicing the new, integrated product development with an initial core team.

The proven toolkit, which is unfortunately all too often neglected, includes, in descending order of effectiveness: the combination of reverse engineering and value engineering; integrated product optimization; parallel development of cost-effective alternatives; design standards and engineering rules; cost catalogs; manufacturability indices; and increased use of identical parts.

Reverse Engineering Combined with Value Engineering

This is probably the most important approach a development team can take to developing cost-efficient products. Applying this approach to one of its products, a domestic appliance manufacturer found that three competing products could be made between 1.3 and 3.5 percent more cheaply. By adopting the more cost-efficient design features—for example, thinner container walls, snap connections instead of screws, simpler cabling, one-piece door seals, and the elimination of unnecessary parts—the company was able to reduce costs for the next product generation by 6.3 percent.

The importance of value engineering seems to be equal in Germany and the United States. Successful companies in both countries claim that about 50 percent of the manufacturing cost reductions achieved result

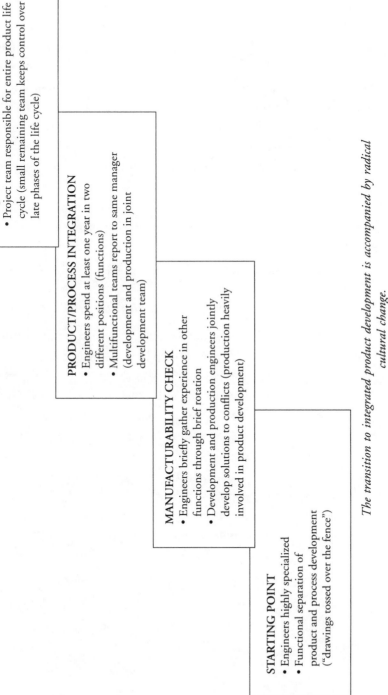

INTEGRATED PRODUCT DEVELOPMENT
• Engineers well trained in many functions
• Project team responsible for entire product life cycle (small remaining team keeps control over late phases of the life cycle)

PRODUCT/PROCESS INTEGRATION
• Engineers spend at least one year in two different positions (functions)
• Multifunctional teams report to same manager (development and production in joint development team)

MANUFACTURABILITY CHECK
• Engineers briefly gather experience in other functions through brief rotation
• Development and production engineers jointly develop solutions to conflicts (production heavily involved in product development)

STARTING POINT
• Engineers highly specialized
• Functional separation of product and process development ("drawings tossed over the fence")

The transition to integrated product development is accompanied by radical cultural change.

Exhibit 3-7. Steps in the Learning Process

from value engineering. The less successful companies in both countries achieve smaller cost reductions and attribute only one-third of the savings on manufacturing costs to value engineering.

Value engineering is not a means of optimizing all the most minute cost factors in a finished product. It is an approach that challenges and optimizes product functions and their production cost as early as the development phase. Half the successful German machinery manufacturers use this method, compared to fewer than one-third of the less successful ones. These companies either prefer to cut costs by trimming the specifications, thereby reducing customer value, or they arrive at a cheaper solution by unsystematic revision of the concept; which typically results in a delayed market launch.

At component manufacturers, whose products often serve only one function, the results of value engineering are less spectacular than among machinery manufacturers, and its application is accordingly less widespread.

Integrated Optimization

A manufacturer of diagnostic equipment saved 6 percent of its production costs when it allowed the cost of the electronic system to rise from 25 percent to 32 percent, but in exchange was able to reduce the mechanical cost from 51 percent to 38 percent of the total. This was achieved by using more sophisticated electronic controls, which, combined with analysis software, helped reduce the number of moving parts in the recording camera.

Such solutions are available only if the entire product development process is integrated. Traditional functional boundaries make it almost impossible to achieve optimization of this kind. Making it work calls for applying it right from the concept phase, ensuring that it includes all subsystems, and setting appropriate tough cost targets for the complete system.

Design Standards and Engineering Rules

At Honda, a maximum of four pressing passes are allowed in the production of exterior body parts. Any deviation from this rule requires the approval of the CEO. European manufacturers, on the other hand, use between six and eight pressing passes for similar parts, which leads to much higher tooling costs and substantial investments in expensive large presses.

Another winning rule is using test criteria that quickly show whether proposed changes in specifications will lead to excessive costs or undesirably long development times. Using such criteria, Japanese companies manage to complete the majority of their design changes very early in the development process. At U.S. manufacturers, by contrast, the greatest number of changes often occur close to production startup. In one case, this difference in approach meant that a Japanese competitor only required a single prototype generation, while a U.S. company needed three.

Cost Catalogs

In selecting the best process, a simple manual of technology-dependent manufacturing costs can be useful, particularly for junior engineers. If the engineer knows, for example, that manual spot welding costs 8 cents per spot and robot spot welding about 3 cents, she will be able to work out roughly what costs her design will generate in production. Such catalogs, with simple key figures, create cost awareness and help the developers achieve the product's cost objectives.

Manufacturability Index

A handy index can help assess how easy individual parts, components, or subsystems are to manufacture. With this approach, if a certain threshold index is not reached, redesign becomes mandatory. After a while, engineers adjust to the manufacturability index's criteria and should, if the criteria have been chosen correctly, be able to design manufacturing-friendly products from the outset.

The value and weighting of manufacturability indices must be individually adapted to the different production processes. Thus, in electronics, the criteria might be the number of standard components used and the number or cost of electrical connections, or the selected component technology (SMD versus PTH). In machinery manufacture, by contrast, the decisive criteria might be the number of different machining stages for individual parts (measured by the number of processes), the number of assembly racks required, or the ratio of catalog parts to special parts.

The impact of simple manufacturability indices is limited, but it can be expanded and enhanced if they are used, for example, to drive the integration of product development. This happens at Hitachi, where the assembly index developed for videorecorder production calls for iterative redesign until a minimum of 80 out of a possible 100 points is achieved. A product optimized in this manner can be produced easily on the existing highly automated assembly line, and the total development time including product/process fit takes only about a year.

Use of Identical Parts

This can be ensured, among other means, by targeted CAD usage. If variants are unavoidable, the main concern should be to introduce variety as late as possible in the production process (e.g., at final assembly) to keep complexity costs low in the early stages (e.g., casting, milling) of the production process, and reduce overall throughput times in production.

Toyota, for example, takes less than a day (two shifts) to move from an engine block casting to a running engine. European competitors need 8 to 15 days for the same process because the larger number of engine variants—which, moreover, arise early in the production process—and the pressure to manufacture these variants in economic quantities lead to sizable buffer inventories between production areas. This not only means higher warehousing and inventory costs, but also conceals mistakes made in the process, which only come to light at the next stage. By contrast, the Japanese approach allows almost inventory-less factories, in which no errors are permitted (or if there are any, they are fixed instantly) during the production process, since they would cause the entire production chain from casting to final assembly to grind to a halt.

All these methods and tools will, however, be largely ineffective unless the total cost is constantly monitored by a transparent system that shows the status of every individual subsystem and allows early remedies if necessary.

✦ ✦ ✦

INTEGRATED PRODUCT DEVELOPMENT holds the potential for significant competitive advantages to be achieved simultaneously in manufacturing and development costs, development time and innovation speed, and development quality. It can weld the management team together in a way no other approach can. However, the transition to integrated product development also requires significant resources, which are best freed up by cancelling marginal projects. This makes development more streamlined and easier to manage. And with the excess weight shed, training for excellence begins.

+ Strategic concentration focuses the entire knowledge and skills of the company on fulfilling the most important customer requirements. Concentrating resources on upstream development ensures largely risk-free downstream work.

+ Elimination and simplification of interfaces are achieved by integrating suppliers and internal functions into product development teams. At the same time, developers come to understand customer value by personal observation, and the scope for action is constantly tested through small innovation steps. Pilot projects offer training opportunities for the team, which will become the nucleus of the new, integrated development group.

+ In internal procedures, short feedback loops drive the constant improvement of product functions and secure the optimum product/process fit.

There seems to be considerable room for German companies to combat overengineering and complexity and reduce manufacturing cost through development. Their U.S. counterparts, on the other hand, appear to be seriously underfunding and understaffing their development efforts, which lead to overly long development times and, even more important, to low product quality.

The successful U.S. companies understand that. There is a good chance that their improved quality products will earn back the respect of the customer and in the long run enable them to achieve price premiums which, together with leaner operations, will result in even better financial results. Those companies that have pursued an undifferentiated cost-cutting approach and are still not able to improve product quality will fail. With merging worldwide competitive focus and buying criteria, the German companies must retain their traditional focus on product quality. But at the same time they need to meet competitive price levels and operating costs through design-to-cost and reducing overengineering and overcomplexity.

The transition to integrated product development can only be achieved step by step. It generally takes more than two product development cycles to complete. Even if the requirements of time and resources seem at first sight to be very high, such a radical change effort of the whole company is unavoidable in many markets. No other approach offers a comparable way to gain the cost, time, and quality improvements made possible by the interaction of customers, marketing, R&D, purchasing, production, sales, service, and suppliers during product development.

FURTHER READING

For a discussion of the innovation curve concept and technology limits, see Richard N. Foster, *Innovation: The Attacker's Advantage* (New York: Summit Books, 1986).

For a discussion of development costs and approaches, see Edward Krubasik, "Customize Your Product Development," *Harvard Business Review*, November–December 1988, p. 46.

For a more detailed discussion of commonality, see John Griffiths, Scott Beardsley, and Robert Kugel, "Commonality: Marrying Design with Process," *The McKinsey Quarterly*, 1991 Number 2, p. 56.

For a discussion of ways to work with suppliers, see Robin Camish and Mark Keough, "A Strategic Role for Purchasing," *The McKinsey Quarterly* 1991, Number 3, p. 22; and Mark Keough, "Buying Your Way to the Top," *The McKinsey Quarterly*, 1993 Number 3, p. 41.

For a detailed discussion of Honda's "expert" system, see Lance Ealey and Leif G. Soderberg, "How Honda Cures 'Design Amnesia,'" *The McKinsey Quarterly*, Spring 1990, p. 3.

4

LOGISTICS

✦ ✦ ✦ ✦ ✦ ✦ ✦ ✦ ✦ ✦ ✦ ✦

Simplicity through Differentiation

A SINGLE product with no customer-specific features or modifications; product documentation so correct and complete that
changes are never necessary; a manufacturing program that remains
unchanged over an extended period; one supplier per component (and
thus fewer suppliers in total, absolutely reliable and punctual); locations
chosen and designed to optimize flows of materials and information; complete freedom from quality defects; information flows that are constantly
clear and up-to-date.

This is how logistics experts might describe the basics of their ideal
world. If it came to pass, not only would they have an easy life, but they
would probably give their company a competitive lead that no one could
catch up with. They would, in fact, be optimizing performance in logistics
(the control of materials and information flows)—an area which accounts
for up to 10 percent of costs in industrial companies. Indeed, logistics has
a major impact on all three dimensions of business performance—cost,
time, and quality (Exhibit 4-1).

This ideal situation may not be fully realized in any company, but
the much-cited "lean" manufacturers of Japan, which have a very good
understanding of exactly what the cost drivers in logistics are, come close.
For one thing, they have consistently opted for a one-product philosophy.
With their luxury-fitted "standard cars," they, unlike their European counterparts, avoid the need for unique, custom-made versions. Where Honda,

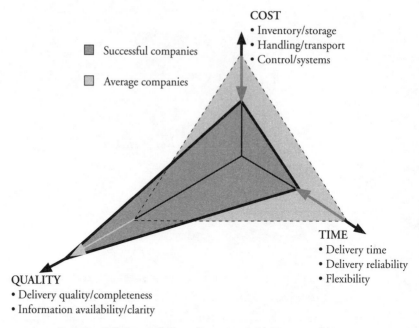

COST
• Inventory/storage
• Handling/transport
• Control/systems

■ Successful companies

□ Average companies

TIME
• Delivery time
• Delivery reliability
• Flexibility

QUALITY
• Delivery quality/completeness
• Information availability/clarity

Logistics influences all three dimensions of business performance.

Exhibit 4-1. Cost, Time, and Quality Impacts of Superior Logistics

for example, manages in some facilities to assemble cars in hourly batches (about 60 per batch), supplying materials turns out to be a relatively simple task. Components, too, can be supplied in batches of 60, transportation containers designed accordingly, assembly sites organized around an hourly rhythm, and the risk of an employee fitting an incorrect component virtually eliminated.

And that's not all. These lean producers also avoid the need for complex input monitoring systems at individual assembly stations, since materials stocks have to meet only one hour's requirements. If products do need to be modified for a particular customer, it can be done as late as possible in the process. Thus all the activities related to order taking, component production, and planning remain "customer-independent" as long as possible.

Lean manufacturing also succeeds outside of Japan. The successful German companies in our survey manage with 20 percent of the product variety that their less successful competitors permit themselves. They source eight out of ten parts from just one supplier, and generally work with only half the number of suppliers that the less successful companies use.

In both the United States and Germany, there seems to be a certain optimum level of supplier concentration. Successful German and U.S. companies single source 85 percent and 75 percent, respectively, of their purchasing volume. Going dramatically lower, say, to 50 percent, single sourcing would not appear to be a good idea, since that is the level of the less successful German companies; but reducing suppliers to a minimum for all purposes could be equally the wrong strategy: the less successful U.S. companies single source as much as 97 percent of their purchasing volume.

In this way the successful companies use logistics to achieve impressive advantages in cost, quality, and—even more significantly—in time. In other words, they achieve a clear superiority in terms of the key buying factors from the customer's point of view: delivery time, delivery accuracy and completeness, and flexibility and information availability throughout an order's progress.

Short delivery times. The successful machinery manufacturers in Germany need just eight weeks on average between receipt of order and delivery; less successful manufacturers take twice as long. Similar differences exist between the successful and less successful component manufacturers, where turnaround times range between four and eight weeks. In the United States, we found that turnarounds of three to four weeks are a prerequisite for competition.

Accurate and complete delivery. Wherever possible, the successful companies complete all orders by the promised deadline in the agreed quantity and quality. Toyota, for example, holds its car component suppliers rigidly to just-in-time delivery. Small parts are supplied to the assembly line twice per shift, large parts up to eight times.

For one U.S. buyer of plant equipment, accurate delivery of spare parts was one of the most important criteria in choosing a European manufacturer. The company's entire plant underwent preventative maintenance at regular four-week intervals. This normally coincided with a planned product changeover, which involved retooling. The supplier that won the order had to guarantee that every spare part needed would be provided on time.

Flexibility and information availability. Successful companies respond flexibly to their customers' demands. They always have up-to-date information about the exact progress of each order. This is extremely valuable to the customer, especially in machinery manufacturing with its relatively long throughput times. In this way, the successful companies meet requests for modification after the initial order without—and this is their real strength—disrupting their own program of purchasing and production.

For each dimension, the successful companies identify the "value thresholds"—the points at which a higher level of service will significantly improve their market competitiveness. But they are equally aware of customer "indifference zones," where a further rise in the level of service will provide little or no additional perceived customer value.

One machinery manufacturer, for example, put a good deal of internal effort into shortening order-processing time by 20 percent. But this achievement was barely noticed by the customer which, knowing that order lead times were relatively long, was only concerned about delivery on a particular day.

By comparison, Caterpillar, one of the world's largest manufacturers of construction equipment, owes its top position to its excellent spare parts service. It guarantees delivery of any type of spare part worldwide within 24 hours. In the construction industry, where business success depends on making optimum use of the operating time of very expensive machines, this is one of the keys to market success.

The successful companies do not, however, obtain their excellent logistics performance at the expense of exorbitant logistics costs. On the contrary, their cost level is often below that of the less successful competitors. In the key functions influenced by logistics, such as purchasing, order processing, materials scheduling and handling, shipping, distribution and receiving, and warehousing, the successful companies in Germany use up to one-third fewer staff; in the United States, the comparable companies use up to two-thirds fewer staff.

Moreover, the German companies' shorter throughput times keep down inventory costs, and their high program stability (low level of disruptions in production) minimizes control and alteration costs. After all, up to 50 percent of logistics costs are generated by unforeseen program changes, which can have an enormous effect on such diverse cost factors as inventory, storage space, capacity utilization, and assembly line input and scheduling. And it is not only the manufacturer that is affected but also often the component supplier.

The successful companies owe their dual advantage—greater customer satisfaction and lower logistics costs—to their superior understanding of the customer, and their clear knowledge of what excellent logistics can contribute toward satisfying customer needs. Not only do they manage well the traditional functional and cross-functional issues related to logistics, they are extremely adept at the strategic dimensions of logistics (Exhibit 4-2).

First, these companies ensure that their location configuration is clear and product-focused. Second, when considering process control within each location, they make a clear distinction between different parts categories and different manufacturing processes.

LOCATION CONFIGURATION: COMBINE WHAT BELONGS TOGETHER

The best logistics performance in terms of both cost and value is achieved by placing the complete "business system" for one product—from development through sales—at a single location, and then focusing that location exclusively on that one product. By doing this, the successful companies gain a clear advantage, thanks to shorter distances, clearer information and material-flows, and fewer frictional losses. Finally, they do not shy away from changing traditional structures—for example, by opting for greenfield expansion.

All Functions under One Roof

Geographical proximity is by no means a panacea. But, by making things simpler physically, it makes an important contribution to efficiency and

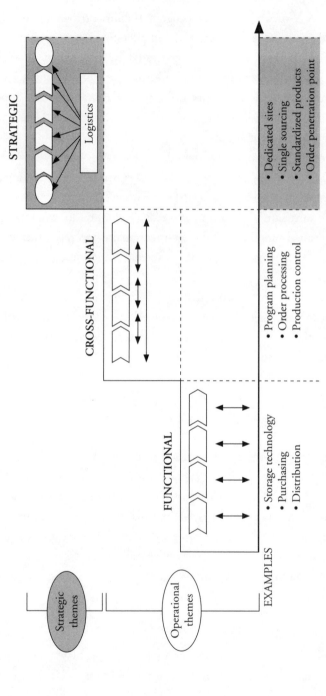

STRATEGIC

CROSS-FUNCTIONAL

FUNCTIONAL

EXAMPLES

Strategic themes

Operational themes

Logistics

- Dedicated sites
- Single sourcing
- Standardized products
- Order penetration point

- Program planning
- Order processing
- Production control

- Storage technology
- Purchasing
- Distribution

The successful companies manage logistics strategically, with a focus on simplicity.

Exhibit 4-2. Different Levels of Logistics Management

effectiveness. If the design department, for example, is a long way from the manufacturing location, communication can be time-consuming and complicated. Even in customized production, where communication needs to be most frequent, such close location is far too seldom the norm. As a result, customers' requests for modifications to their order remain unattended to for far too long. And poor information flows can prevent ideas from design being harnessed to maximize manufacturing efficiency.

It is equally important, especially in machinery manufacture, for design and sales to be close together. One company discovered just how important this is when it spent years trying unsuccessfully to overcome its problems with delivery times and reliability. Analysis revealed the main cause of the problems. The sales department concentrated exclusively on getting the customer to sign the order, and so the sales function was largely cut off from the internal flow of information. As a result, orders omitted a number of technical details that were important for both design and production.

When the signed but incomplete order was passed on to the design department, long and complex discussions became necessary. These were conducted in part by telephone, in part by letter, and in part by personal contact between the designer and the customer. With an average agreed-on delivery time of four months, orders were often processed under great time pressure, and it was hardly surprising that the company achieved only a suboptimal 80 percent delivery reliability.

When the central sales department subsequently moved to the design and production site, there was an almost immediate noticeable improvement. Staff from sales and design learned from personal contact with one another how they could make each other's work easier and more effective. Working together, they produced a comprehensive, standardized quotation form, laying out in clear "modules" the most important technical information needed from the customer. The result was a detailed document for each order, containing all the essential information. The lengthy after-sales discussion and clarification, which had hitherto been a fixed feature of the development work, could be eliminated. Throughput time was cut by more than half.

The sales function itself benefited, too. Thanks to the comprehensive and quickly compiled information (the documents were stored on computer in the form of text modules), sales was able to provide customers with a comprehensive quotation within a few hours, even for complex requests. Customers were impressed by the amount of information included in their quotation and found that it helped them identify their needs early on.

One Product, One Factory

The successful companies establish a single location for each product or product group, while the less successful companies opt for several smaller sites producing the same or similar product combinations. The advantage of the simpler structure, as far as the successful companies are concerned, is that everything is easier to understand, especially the core processes and the key levers in each part of the business system. By focusing on one product and its strengths, the companies can make rapid decisions at all levels (from top management to the individual at the machine), and successfully implement strategies and improvement programs.

The successful companies take specialization or differentiation still further as and when the nature of the product range dictates. One very successful manufacturer of large plant machinery, for example, decided to build a new factory for one product line that had become increasingly customer-specific over time. Unlike the rest of the product group, which continued to be mass produced, here it was necessary to respond precisely to specific customer requests for design modifications to each order. Lot sizes fell, more and more order-specific parts were necessary, frequent customer-specific changes were common. Even though the products were still similar, a completely different business system had evolved.

This "alien" part of the business was moved in its entirety to the new factory, which, like the main plant, encompassed all functions from development, through component manufacture and assembly, to sales. The investment was worthwhile because it avoided the dissipation of effort that can come from mixing large-scale and custom-made production in each of the functions—and, more important, in the minds of staff, in systems and in production technology.

Even within individual sites, differentiation is possible in response to differing needs for flows of information and materials. Among the successful companies, the individual plant's machine shops can become a "factory within a factory." In such cases, it is not enough simply to focus the production technology on each particular subassembly or component group. Planning and control activities also need to be adapted to the individual plant and its products. Thus, for example, a single site can include one plant dedicated to mass production next to another, more flexible plant that handles custom orders, small batches, or C components.

More and more companies are striving to separate mass production from customized production, whether at the plant level (i.e., through a dedicated plant within a site) or by simply devoting an entire location to a specific product. Where, because of the breadth of products, it is not possible to differentiate between mass and customized production, as is frequently the case with manufacturers of highly customer-specific machinery, the successful companies apply the factory-within-a-factory concept to individual product groups or components.

The factory-within-a-factory is not limited to one process, such as turning, milling, or sheet-metal processing. Instead it is responsible for the complete production of one subassembly. In this "island" arrangement, focused on components or subassemblies, the leader or the foreman (*Meister*) not only has more responsibility, but also enjoys a better overview and greater influence over cost, time, and quality targets.

The successful companies recognize that differentiation, whether between mass and customized production or between separate components/subassemblies, not only minimizes setup and control costs. It also increases motivation and performance among staff, since they gain more responsibility for areas of activity within their control and can make better decisions. The companies found that in every single case productivity increased measurably at the respective site or plant.

Radical Greenfield Solutions

According to our survey, half of the successful companies were operating out of locations that they had built in the past five to ten years. By contrast, only one in ten of the less successful companies took this step; 70 percent remained on their traditional production site; and 20 percent had a location configuration that was a direct result of acquisitions of other companies. We found a similar trend in the United States, where up to 40 percent of the companies had invested in greenfield sites in the last five years.

This confirms the fact that it is typically the most successful companies that are willing to expand into greenfield sites, in order to optimize the flow of materials and information and achieve the kind of differentiation we have been describing. The catalyst for this move can—but need not necessarily—be a surge of growth or a broadening of the product range. And an important consideration in the final choice of site is the supply of labor in the region.

If a greenfield solution is to realize its full value in logistics terms, the aim should not be merely to use new, faster machines to shorten actual processing time. Rather, it should be to accelerate and simplify the flow of materials and information. The benefit of such an approach is exemplified by a machinery manufacturer which, when building a new factory, invested in a computer-aided, automated guided vehicle system.

In the company's newly constructed small-components plant, which handled a multiplicity of parts, the computerized system was used to keep the machines supplied with work. But the large investment involved would not have been justified purely by the reduction in the number of forklift truck drivers made possible by automation. Systematic use of the new technology in production control gave rise to many additional benefits.

The zones reserved for materials delivery in front of each machine were kept small, and the supply of work was limited to three pallets' worth—equivalent to about two hours' work. Similarly, the area set aside for finished parts accommodated just three pallets. No additional space was available in front of or behind the machine, to avoid blocking the path of the automated vehicles. This "enforced order" ensured that operators at each machine gave parts orders on time. And the limited supply of work made them adhere strictly to the appropriate machining sequence. In addition, inventory levels in this plant remained extremely low.

While the immediately visible benefit of investing in automated vehicles was to minimize transport/handling costs, far more significant was the reduction in throughput times and the minimization of control costs. All in all, it proved far better to start from scratch than to attempt incremental improvement of the existing structure—for example, by investing in tooling technology or improved production control.

In another successful example, an entire new factory was equipped for kanban production, again with the goal of minimizing throughput times and control costs. Thanks to a product redesign, the parts involved were relatively few, the production batches from one stage to the next were identical, and relatively small load carriers could be used. As a result, throughput times were extremely short and there was no need for computer systems to fine-tune production.

DIFFERENTIATED PROCESS CONTROL

Just as it makes sense to specialize locations by product, in process control it pays to be more precise about different parts categories and manufacturing processes. The apparently "simple" principle of treating everything in the same way should be abandoned. Simplicity, and the resulting time and and cost savings, can be achieved much more effectively by combining like with like and giving them the same treatment, and by differentiating precisely between various types of products, parts, and processes.

Such strict differentiation reduces both volume and complexity. This can be seen very clearly in purchasing logistics. Purchasing for a machinery or component manufacturer typically involves about 3,000 to 8,000 part numbers. If one attempted to optimize, for the complete range of A components to C components, every logistics-related factor (inventory costs, ordering costs, handling costs, and so on), the resulting complexity would be prohibitively expensive and virtually impossible to master, even with the most elaborate systems. A far more effective approach is to identify the key variable for each component type and optimize that.

Similarly, in production logistics, simplicity and efficiency can be achieved by focusing control on program and process stability.

Minimize A components inventory and C components handling: Analyses of parts purchasing usually shows that between 10 and 20 percent of all supplied components account for more than 80 percent of procurement value, and give rise to correspondingly high inventory costs. For these parts, high availability must be guaranteed, while inventory costs must be minimized.

At the other extreme, with C components (generally up to 80 percent of all supplied parts), inventory costs are often negligible. These seldom-used parts often account for just 15 to 20 percent of the value of all materials and fuel. Nevertheless, adequate stocks have to be held to ensure their availability when needed. The main logistics costs here arise from handling, given the large number of parts. Irrespective of volume, these parts incur transportation costs: they must be unloaded, pass through incoming goods inspection (at least for identification), and be moved into and stored in the warehouse. Normally it is not possible to take C components straight past inspection to where they are needed in production or assembly. There is no guarantee that they will be needed regularly, and parts ordering is typically dictated by a "safe inventory level" set by a central warehouse.

Successful companies in Germany, however, differentiate according to the following logistics typology. For A components with high turnover and value, they try to keep inventory costs low. They place orders weekly, in some cases daily or even hourly. Because of this order frequency, their inventory reach amounts to about 20 days. With the more numerous C components (the less frequently used parts), the companies focus on reducing handling costs—in ordering, incoming goods, and warehouse handling. For these parts, the companies deliberately aim for an average inventory reach of up to 180 working days, and place orders only at one-, three-, or six-month intervals. This means that the cost of tying up capital and the cost of storage space are slightly higher, but handling costs are minimized, as is the risk of stockouts, which can lead to high consequential costs (Exhibit 4-3).

The less successful companies do not recognize the importance of differentiating between the different component types. Because they do not establish simple priorities, their purchasing departments have to manage the costs of ordering, handling, and storage, as well as the risk of stockouts, for the entire component range.

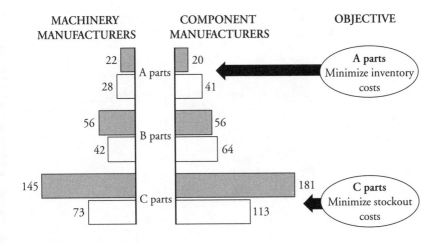

| MACHINERY MANUFACTURERS | COMPONENT MANUFACTURERS | OBJECTIVE |

■ Successful companies   □ Less successful companies

In purchasing logistics, the successful companies differentiate clearly between A and C parts.

Exhibit 4-3. Inventory Levels for Components (production days, 1989)

In one company with small-batch production, for example, almost the entire range of components needed for production was delivered at two- to three-week intervals. As a result, enormous peaks affected every function—incoming goods, handling, and storage. Suppliers and transporters resented long waiting times when delivering, and the company had relatively long inventory reaches and, because of the peaks, correspondingly high handling costs.

By differentiating by component type, the company was able to reduce its logistics costs drastically and improve the quality of service to the production function. For A components it increased delivery frequency—to weekly, every second day, or daily—while for C components it extended its order cycle to two-month and sometimes four-month delivery. A relatively simple computer system now ensures that parts are re-ordered as soon as they fall below safe inventory levels, and it also makes it easier (or even unnecessary) for purchasing to keep track of the numerous C components. Instead, purchasing can now focus on the critical A components—for example, by introducing just-in-time delivery. Stockouts have been virtually eliminated.

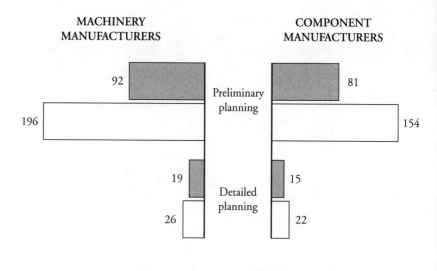

The successful companies achieve high program stability by means of shorter planning horizons.

Exhibit 4-4. Time Horizons for Short- and Long-Range Planning (working days)

Program Stability: Discipline at Every Level

Because of their tight planning horizons, the successful companies need to make fewer program changes than their less successful competitors. In particular, they base their long-range production plans on much shorter time horizons, which they then adhere to strictly.

By keeping their time horizons, especially for long-term planning, much shorter than their less successful competitors, the successful companies manage to retain the necessary overview with flexibility to make changes. Thus they avoid the vicious cycle in which long throughput times are translated into long planning horizons, and every modification causes extensive program changes. By comparison, the longer-range planning in the less successful companies is constantly subjected to alteration and ties up considerably more planning capacity (Exhibit 4-4).

But that is not all. The successful companies also manage to control the other factors that influence program stability, not least the sales department's ability to plan precisely. And they are quick to recognize when program stability is at risk. This can happen, for example, if there are constant last-minute changes to the monthly program (in terms of quantities, sequence, or products), leading in turn to inadequate lead times for production, program changes, and late deliveries.

To solve this kind of problem, the successful companies employ simple measures—whether systems-related, organizational, or operational.

+ Systems measures. Unlike many companies which base their program planning on past observation extrapolated (with some modification) into the future, the successful companies use more effective instruments. Often it is sufficient simply to adopt different planning methods or frequencies at different times of the year. A consumer goods manufacturer, for example, might normally use regression techniques, but would use different planning instruments when seasonal peaks or price increases were expected.

   If planning cycles in the various parts of a company are not synchronized, demand patterns can become severely distorted. At one component manufacturer, for example, monthly demand from the sales offices for common replacement parts was almost invariable. However, since each sales office had its own rhythm, the central warehouse built up a very uneven picture for the individual months. The central warehouse, in turn, passed the orders on to production to suit its own rhythm. This produced highly irregular production figures over the year. In the end, the company managed to smooth these irregularities out simply by synchronizing the planning cycles: it collected all the orders from the market (via the sales offices) at the same time and passed them directly on to production.

+ Organizational measures. In some cases—particularly in specialized machinery production—program stability cannot be achieved by introducing systems. Instead, organizational measures are needed. A properly staffed order-handling unit with the necessary skills can provide very effective logistics coordination between all the functions in a business. This unit's flexibility allows it to meet the most wide-ranging needs, priorities, and requests for modification, no matter where they come from—sales, customized design, materials management, production, or assembly.

Such a unit is in a better position than the functional departments to guarantee the fastest possible order throughput, since it can redefine and then monitor the rules of the game for the individual functions, particularly regarding delivery reliability. And by seeing the "big picture," it can point out repercussions (for example, when delivery dates are put back) and prioritize the order sequence. Many companies still try in vain to achieve the discipline of an order-handling unit by introducing costly, complex, and usually ineffective systems.

♦ Operational measures. Short-term program stability can also be achieved by operational measures—that is, by direct intervention in production. For example, Japanese car manufacturers often build in buffers of two to four hours between the early and the late shift. Such buffers provide an opportunity for catching up, if one area of production has fallen behind its daily quota. The two-hour buffer is almost always sufficient to get production in each area back on schedule in time for the next shift.

In addition, any maintenance work that could not be completed during the first shift, including preventative measures aimed at avoiding machine breakdown, can be carried out between the first and the second shift, thus avoiding production standstills in the late shift. This leads to higher labor productivity: on the one hand, machine operators can achieve optimal volumes since there are almost no interruptions; on the other hand, maintenance staff can thoroughly prepare themselves and concentrate on their work during the two extra hours.

The primary aim of this arrangement is high process and program stability. Japanese companies have long since recognized the beneficial effects of such stability on logistics performance and have organized their production in this simple way.

Process Stability Depends on Work Sequence and Control Responsibility

Process stability is a function of a number of factors, including large production runs, minimal downtime, minimum setup time, high machine time availability, and therefore high labor productivity. Several logistics parameters can help achieve or guarantee the required process stability in production. An optimized inventory level at the individual machine, production control and sequence planning "close to the action," and streamlined and transparent materials flows can all have a significant impact.

Although production itself is often the lengthiest part of the process a product undergoes, in many companies it is nevertheless still something of a "black box." This must be the explanation for the fact that often only one-tenth of total throughput time is spent strictly in production—the remaining 90 percent is primarily waiting time.

In companies where "one or two production steps per week" is normal (as in many companies that manufacture products individually), this can rarely be put down to careless machine operation, low productivity, or poor parts availability. On the contrary, it is often because production is oversupplied with materials. In practice, the amount of work waiting to be done at each machine is so large that the operator can no longer tell which orders have the highest priority. And the control function is equally in the dark. If the build-up of work at the machines amounts to 20 days on average, which is often the case in the less successful German machinery companies, then extended throughput times are inevitable (Exhibit 4-5).

By contrast, the successful German machinery companies reduce work build-ups to two days on average—either through assembly-related changes and supporting systems (as in the example of the automated guided vehicle system described above), or through other control measures. This still leaves machine operators enough flexibility to sequence their work effectively or to fit in maintenance work. The low levels of inventory provide the control function with sufficient "transparency" to plan for short throughput times and to spot and deal with problems early on.

The successful machinery and component manufacturers also take organizational measures to ensure process stability—by locating responsibility for control at the most suitable vantage point. Thus, the successful German machinery manufacturers give responsibility for detailed job sequence decisions to the foreman, while among the less successful companies (in four out of five cases), individual parts production is controlled centrally or at the level of the individual production zone.

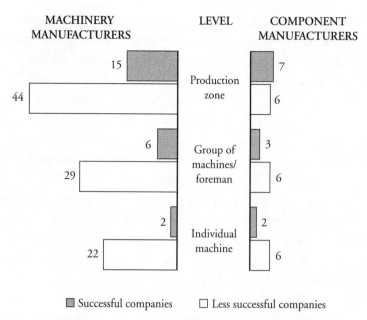

MACHINERY MANUFACTURERS		LEVEL	COMPONENT MANUFACTURERS	
15		Production zone	7	
44			6	
6		Group of machines/ foreman	3	
29			6	
2		Individual machine	2	
22			6	

■ Successful companies   □ Less successful companies

The key to effective production process is adhering to the planned sequence.
Exhibit 4-5. Work Reserves in Production (working days)

Among the German component manufacturers, whose production runs are mainly high volume, these ratios are reversed: 80 percent of the successful companies control at the individual production zone level or higher, giving the foreman no responsibility for control. Among the less successful companies, up to 20 percent allow the foreman control responsibility.

The same rule applies in principle to both machinery manufacturers and component manufacturers: fine control should be located as decentrally as possible. It is far easier to know what is really going on, to distinguish between competing orders, and to know which problems occur again and again, if one is at the production zone level. Planning and control systems can then provide helpful support, provided they leave the person in control enough room for discretion.

✦ ✦ ✦

LOGISTICS ACCOUNTS FOR as much as 10 percent of total costs in industrial companies. Moreover, logistics performance—that is, the control of materials and information flows—also has a direct bearing on the level of service provided to the customer: delivery times, reliability, and flexibility. It follows that optimizing logistics performance means achieving the maximum level of service at the lowest possible cost. When the successful companies manage delivery times of 8 weeks compared with 16 weeks (often with higher logistics costs) for their less successful competitors, it becomes clear just how much improvement potential lies dormant.

The key lessons here are:

+ Strategic concentration means focusing on "value thresholds." Delivery times, reliability, and flexibility with respect to customers' alteration requests should be improved *only* where the customer perceives and is willing to pay for additional value. Equally important, service levels should *not* be improved if they are unimportant to the customer.

+ Elimination and simplification of interfaces are achieved above all by focusing locations on products. Wherever possible, a single location per product or product line should be established, encompassing all the functions necessary to process orders optimally. Greenfield solutions should be adopted where appropriate.

+ In internal procedures, different logistics solutions should be used for different parts categories. For A parts, the priority is to minimize inventory. This can be achieved through high program stability, which in turn depends on process stability, strict adherence to work sequences, and clearly delegated responsibility for control. For C parts, on the other hand, the emphasis should be placed on minimizing handling.

Experience suggests that modifications to logistics procedures of the kind described here can be achieved relatively quickly, within six to twelve months.

5

TECHNOLOGY

✦ ✦ ✦ ✦ ✦ ✦ ✦ ✦ ✦ ✦ ✦ ✦ ✦

Simplification before Automation

O R more than a decade, the fast pace and direction of productivity improvements have been set by computer-assisted flexible automation. Computer support, from central DP through CAD to CNC machines and MRP systems, is now an accepted integral part of everyday business life.

Yet how such technology is used is still subject to debate. For one thing, there is no sight like hindsight—and lessons for the future can and should be learned from using it. For another, our survey of machinery and component manufacturers shed some more light on how the use of computer technologies can contribute to a competence-based competitive edge.

The last wave of automation ebbed to reveal the success—as well as a good many failures—of many investments in technology. Companies are becoming disillusioned. Although German manufacturers have in many cases automated more individual processes and have spent far more on information technology, Japanese competitors are between two and four times as productive. A prime example is final assembly in the automotive industry.

Similar developments can be observed in industry in general. The successful German machinery manufacturers spend just over one-third of the less successful companies' total on IT, or 1.4 percent of sales. This saving alone—about 2.5 percent of sales—is enough to make the difference between a mediocre and a flourishing company. But the successful compa-

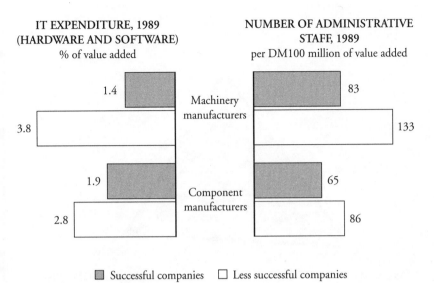

IT EXPENDITURE, 1989
(HARDWARE AND SOFTWARE)
% of value added

NUMBER OF ADMINISTRATIVE
STAFF, 1989
per DM100 million of value added

Machinery
manufacturers

1.4

3.8

83

133

Component
manufacturers

1.9

2.8

65

86

■ Successful companies   □ Less successful companies

Successful companies achieve higher productivity in administration with less IT.

Exhibit 5-1. IT Expenditure and Administrative Productivity

nies are more efficient as well: their personnel productivity—in administration, for example—is more than 30 percent higher (Exhibit 5-1).

Those companies that take a cautious approach to automation achieve
their productivity gains from better product design, better management
of complexity, far more efficient procedures, and, above all, stable processes. It seems likely that the rush into automation has actually been partly
responsible for the neglect of these simple improvement opportunities in
Europe—and for some time in the United States. The new technologies
were regarded as *the* way to achieve higher productivity at any desired level
of complexity. This often led to the introduction of unstable processes
within complex environments, causing considerable disruption to the system as a whole.

Of course, complete avoidance of automation is not the answer either.
The Japanese, among others, are intensely preoccupied with new opportunities derived from computer technologies. Indeed, it is likely to be the
Japanese, building on controlled processes and simple environments, who
will push automation step by step in the future to achieve the next quan-

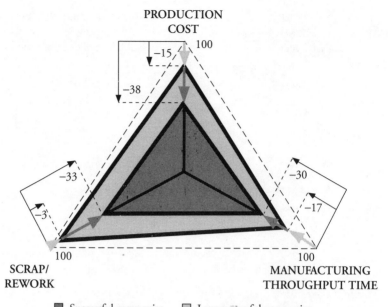

PRODUCTION
COST

SCRAP/
REWORK

MANUFACTURING
THROUGHPUT TIME

■ Successful companies   □ Less successful companies

Successful companies obtain significantly higher value with computer technologies.

Exhibit 5-2. Average Improvement from CAM Introduction, 1985–1989 (% of starting value)

tum leap in productivity. For all their restraint in IT, the successful machinery and component manufacturers in Germany estimate that they have achieved cost, time, and quality improvements of about 30 percent within five years through computer technologies. The fact that the less successful companies (with more new technology) improved by only about 10 percent in the same period simply confirms how important it is to invest wisely in this area (Exhibit 5-2).

We now know what it takes to succeed. Above all else, get the strategic focus right. The following case—somewhat exaggerated, but not that far from the truth—illustrates why.

Returning from a conference, the marketing VP is enthusiastic about "lot sizes of one." Can the company finally get its own production people to look into this concept, which appears to be industry standard nowadays? The production VP thinks marketing has given orders for total flexibility, which he reckons can only be achieved with highly flexible manufacturing systems. The materials management VP is tired of being constantly blamed for stockouts which, as far as he is concerned, are primarily due to regular planning changes rather than to poor supplier management. He puts in a bid for an integrated sales forecasting, capacity planning, and materials management system.

All these objectives are understandable from the point of view of the requestor, and are logical enough in themselves. But put into practice, they would lead to disaster. A lot size of one requirement in manufacturing leads to investments frequently two to four times those needed for a simple transfer line or a standard machining center. And the productivity of direct (machine operators) and indirect (maintenance, quality assurance, and so on) labor is halved at best, even with highly productive equipment. High-tech systems typically have much longer downtimes than relatively simple, single-purpose machinery.

As a result, in no time at all the total cost level would be at least 30 percent above best practice. If the product is one where the customer is chiefly interested in low cost, so that the price premiums for special solutions are low, the company would be busily working its way into a totally uncompetitive position, particularly in the volume segment. In more or less extreme forms, this pattern is fairly well established at the less successful companies.

To be genuinely effective, technology must be applied—as with other elements of the business—in such a way as to create real customer value. The key is to find out what the customer really wants, and, as with product-range and development strategies, to identify breakpoints: improvements that give customers a fundamental advantage, and for which they are therefore prepared to pay a substantial premium. One question steers the discussion about automation in the right direction: How can a company achieve competitive differentiation by making the transition to a new breakpoint?

For component manufacturers, the breakpoint is generally a cost parameter, and the use of computer technologies plays a subordinate role. Even today, rigid transfer lines are often still the most efficient way to produce high daily unit outputs, and systems requirements can be kept within reasonable bounds with simple process structures.

This approach—consistently subordinating the discussion of automation to the development of an integrated concept—came up some years ago, when we discussed production automation strategies with leading Japanese companies. At first, they did not seem to understand the point of the question. In the politest possible way, they steered the conversation toward the subject of productivity improvement, since the industry was mainly cost driven, and breakpoints could only come in the form of cost advantages. Much of the time was spent discussing how to establish the conditions for designing simpler products, how to implement the corresponding organizational changes, and how to design programs for overall productivity improvement. All this was a prologue to considering the role computer technologies might play in this context.

A clear understanding of the breakpoint concept is the core of every effective computer technology strategy. As with all the activities of the successful companies, the key is to follow the rules of simplicity in concept and implementation:

+ First of all, simplify rigorously. Use technology to perform simple, manageable tasks as efficiently as possible, rather than to manage overcomplexity.

+ Then introduce targeted automation. Invest heavily in well-understood technologies, and experiment selectively with pioneering solutions.

SIMPLICITY RULES

To add a good cost position to its defenses against Asian competitors, a Western computer manufacturer developed a new printer especially designed for fully automatic assembly. Considerable resources had been invested in the project, and it would probably have been celebrated as a major success story—had not sales suddenly collapsed for reasons totally unconnected with automation.

In this crisis, the company played through every action scenario, including transferring to manual assembly below certain unit-production levels. The manual option proved to be very straightforward, since the assembly processes had been radically simplified for the purposes of automation. Closer inspection revealed that the high level of automation had never been economically viable, and was all the less so at lower production levels. Notwithstanding the residual fixed cost, all production was therefore transferred to manual assembly.

Rigorous simplification does not always make computer technologies redundant. But automation should not be introduced until opportunities for improving efficiency through simplification have been exhaustively explored. That is the point where computer technologies become both effective and cost-efficient.

Fostering simplicity in technology starts with simple product concepts that facilitate automation and keep related investment within reasonable bounds. But simple structures, simple machinery, and simple systems are at least equally important.

Simple Product Concepts

Attempts to automate products designed for shop manufacture typically lead either to quite excessive investments or to the conclusion that it cannot be done. Neither outcome is acceptable—or necessary, as the success of companies from our survey illustrated. Successful machinery manufacturers, for example, use CAD extensively only if there is considerable potential for product standardization. Otherwise, they steer well clear of it. The less successful companies take a quite different approach. When product complexity is high, they try to use CAD to control it; when product complexity is low, they think they have everything under control, and therefore use CAD less. Their average return on sales, at 2.3 percent, is at least 50 percent lower than even that of companies that have neither standardized, nor attempted to automate complexity.

As the successful machinery makers know, a CAD system may be no more than an electronic pencil when used to design nonstandardized products. The designer may achieve, at best, 30 to 50 percent higher productivity than with a traditional drawing board, but will, more often than not, achieve no improvement at all. By contrast, higher standardization may increase productivity by a factor of 3 to 4 in design engineering alone. The figures are even more extreme at plant construction companies, which, with proper standardization, can prepare their bidding documents five to six times faster: five weeks cut to five days is regarded as normal.

Similar effects can be achieved for cutting operations on transfer lines. One German manufacturer had high product variety and therefore needed very complex machinery, which was not only extremely expensive, but extremely prone to breakdowns. The company's Japanese competitors, by contrast, had been able to limit the differences between variants on one line to only four borehole diameters and depths.

Requiring just half the investment of the German company, the Japanese firm managed to reduce setup times and equipment sensitivity to such an extent that it now has a yield of 85 percent, while the highly complex German plant manages 55 percent at best. In addition, the Japanese company operates its plant with about one-third of the manpower. The total cost per item machined is thus about 60 percent lower, a gap that can only be closed by intelligent—simple—product design.

An example from machinery manufacture provides a very clear illustration of the link between standardization and automation. The company decided in the early 1980s to set up a greenfield factory, in order, among other reasons, to have the freedom to install full automation. This factory was intended not only to have automatic machining and handling, but also wherever possible an automatic information flow. Despite generous investment in plant and systems, production startup kept going wrong. Some system was always breaking down, more coordination was needed between individual elements than expected, and cost and time targets were far from being met.

The management team reviewed the overall concept, and found that automating the existing, highly complex product range could not possibly produce the desired results. Subsequent radical product standardization reduced the variety of components significantly, and clever product design deferred remaining complexity to a late phase in the assembly process.

But management went a step further. It differentiated manufacturing by splitting the production program clearly into "volume" and "exotic" lines. That made it possible to get maximum productivity for the high-volume products with extremely simple processes and structures, while accepting high setup and learning times for the exotic lines.

Overall, a simple product concept, combined with modifications in structures and procedures, allowed a dramatic reduction in computerization and much better machine concepts.

Simple Structures

However important product standardization may be, the biggest obstacle to automation (particularly in the systems area) lies in the philosophy of central management and control. Years of experience have led many companies to believe that it is impossible to do advance scheduling for complex manufacturing and then assume that everything will go as planned. These companies know that suppliers simply cannot avoid the occasional delivery bottleneck, and that breakdowns in upstream operations can play havoc with production plans. So they design systems that take day-to-day glitches into account, and can respond to such problems with centralized rescheduling.

But even such practice-oriented systems design has proved to be a recipe for chaos. The Japanese take a different approach: they create clear structures and assign responsibilities; they give the responsible managers freedom in reaching objectives; and they ensure that variances do not happen.

Imagine that a highly complex, fully integrated logistics system had been created for the automotive industry, with everything from medium-term program planning to fine-tuning targeted to a just-in-time system. At first sight, of course, this "intelligent" system would seem superior. Only one master production schedule would be drawn up—a "feasible" schedule, taking into account both manpower and machine capacity.

In theory, the system's impact would be enormous; perfect accuracy in the production program would capture dramatic productivity improvement potential. The direct cost of stockouts, which lead to pulling cars off the line, is very high; moreover, additional costs arise which can easily amount to 20 or 30 percent of manufacturing cost; and then there are the inevitable quality problems.

On closer examination, however, it becomes clear that the supersystem would have to coordinate an infinite number of parameters if it were to calculate a new optimum for the entire company every time something changed. And since there will always be a machine down somewhere, or more workers will be off sick or returning to work than expected, the system would be highly unstable.

This becomes particularly clear from a simple, though fictitious, example. If an upstream operation suddenly suffers a break in delivery from its steel manufacturer, the system will immediately realize that a certain component will be unavailable. From this, it will determine what changes will be necessary in the production program to maintain continued delivery capability. A highly intelligent system would also determine the appropriate direct action—giving rise to problems at every other stage. It would again base its calculations on theoretically available capacities, whereas the required capacity might not actually be available on the days concerned. Such a situation would not even have been regarded as critical in the original program, since the plant manager would undoubtedly have known how to complete the delayed program.

If, by contrast, we take a "dumb" system and simply assume that the upstream operation will deliver as planned, systems devotees will expect more disruption of supply than before. Experience, however, shows the opposite. In real life, the plant manager affected by the supply-chain disruption will probably find ways to produce the parts despite the problems. He may be able to find another material, which could mean higher costs, but will maintain delivery capability. And his entrepreneurial spirit will drive him to try and obtain the material, either from another supplier or, in extreme cases, from a competitor.

Apart from the fact that a plant manager will probably be better able to control this isolated problem than an integrated system, the decentralized approach has another advantage—probably the most important. The manager of the upstream operation will probably make a deal with the supplier who caused the disruption to bear the extra costs, which in turn will deter the supplier from allowing similar problems to occur in the future. Moreover, the manager will make it clear to the supplier that disruptions are unacceptable and that purchasing and development may not renew the supplier's contract. Alternatively, he will cooperate with the supplier to find ways to prevent supply problems.

In the highly complex system, by contrast, the problem will not be immediately apparent in most cases. The system will perform the rescheduling, the plant manager will never find out what caused the rescheduling, and all will be well with the upstream operation, too, since it will probably be producing as closely as possible according to the program. Trouble will occur only at the other production facilities, where actual and theoretical capacity were not identical. But these plant managers, too, will have almost no room for maneuver, since they will see the system's last-minute intervention as erratic and impossible to influence.

Clear structures and objectives are an essential prerequisite for successful production and automation. Instead of planning and controlling every detail centrally, management usually installs independent cost or profit centers, individually responsible for optimizing cost, throughput times/parts availability, and quality.

Simple Machinery and Systems

Once the right environmental conditions have been set up with simple product concepts and structures, systems and equipment can also be designed much more simply, as demonstrated in the transfer line example.

Systems support: Simplicity of systems support is inseparably linked with the issues of centralization or decentralization, integration or stand-alone solutions. Centralized supersystems typically do not leave managers enough flexibility to achieve their objectives. Yet it is just as dangerous to allow systems to become totally separated. The successful companies tend to prefer a certain degree of drifting apart to being overregimented. They foster extensive automation of individual divisions or elements before introducing fully integrated process chains.

The successful companies make individual operating units responsible for their own IT projects. At less successful companies, on the other hand, ultimate responsibility often lies with the central IT department. As a result, less successful companies attribute considerable significance to companywide standard approaches in IT projects, while the successful companies do not think they matter (Exhibit 5-3).

Successful companies limit integration to the few really critical tasks. Even then, their first question is whether systems are needed for integra-

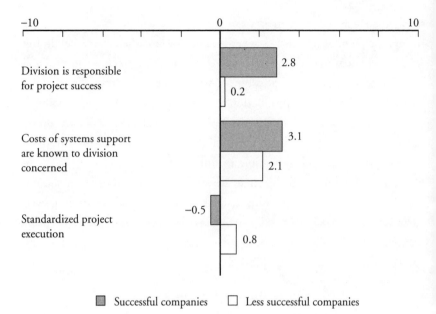

| | −10 | 0 | 10 |

Division is responsible for project success
2.8
0.2

Costs of systems support are known to division concerned
3.1
2.1

Standardized project execution
−0.5
0.8

■ Successful companies   □ Less successful companies

Successful companies emphasize divisional responsibility when introducing IT systems.

Exhibit 5-3. Approach to IT Systems Introduction (scalar rankings)

tion, or whether it is better accomplished by individual people or structures. Their motto is "Think big, act small." So, although they keep the big picture in mind and define the systems architecture in such a way as to facilitate future integration—where it is useful and necessary—they ensure that major benefits are achieved up front from optimizing small areas.

The dangers of overcentralization contrasted with the benefits of a more decentralized approach were experienced directly by one major machinery manufacturer. At the start of the 1980s, management was planning to introduce a fully integrated production and inventory control (MRP II) system. The system was based directly on development's bill of materials, but also made direct use of the sales forecast. Although the main factory introduced this theoretically superior system, a smaller facility opted for a different solution. In place of the integrated system, it wanted to start with a simple standard product-scheduling software package—

with all the necessary business-specific adaptations—with a view to making the transition as soon as the integrated system had proved itself.

The progress of the two systems to date is highly instructive. In the main factory, launch dates have been postponed again and again. Although the system was supposed to be in full operation within two years at the latest, no one takes this target seriously, since the same thing has been said since the project began. The effort has been a disaster. In the main factory, the old semimanual systems are still in operation. Assuming that the new MRP II system would solve all its problems, the company has not even begun the essential systematic simplification of planning and control procedures and product structuring. This is one of the main reasons why costs in parts manufacturing are 40 percent higher than in comparable production facilities.

The small facility, by contrast, introduced its simple production-scheduling system relatively early and fast. The theoretical disadvantage—that the system is not integrated with the sales forecast—has actually been turned into an advantage. Constantly corrected sales forecasts would have necessitated day-to-day rescheduling. The facility has, however, restructured its products to form families of parts. This allows most fluctuations in the product mix to be absorbed relatively easily in production.

The integration of consumption forecasts with the production-scheduling system by means of an intelligent filter—in this case, a member of staff—works much better than the data transfer method, which may be more efficient but causes confusion in production.

The smaller facility has achieved a highly competitive cost position. About eight years ago it was still thought of as one of the firm's problem factories; it is now the jewel in the crown. Naturally, no one suggests that it was the production-scheduling system that solved all the problems. Management is more likely to emphasize the families of parts, flow manufacturing, greater staff motivation, and higher machine utilization. But the fact that the facility was able to design the system and the aggregation of orders without rigid top-down instructions opened up opportunities for highly efficient operations overall.

In the main factory, on the other hand, plant management was bound to the specifications of the highly intelligent MRP II system. Interim solutions were not allowed; they were thought likely to cause problems later for the integrated supersystem and therefore to be avoided at all costs—with the results outlined above.

The considerable risks of both overcentralization and overdecentralization can often be seen in the use of CAD. Although some companies have handed over decisions on CAD systems to the divisions, without laying down common policies of any kind, others have prescribed that only specified hardware and software be used, with very tight centralized control.

Neither solution has proved satisfactory. With the overdecentralized approach, subsequent networking/integration has proved difficult and complex. The overcentralized approach, on the other hand, has blocked important decision making. The integration problem is undoubtedly the lesser of the two evils. But there is a better solution: prescribe a systems architecture centrally and secure certain interfaces, and leave the user complete freedom in selecting applications software.

Even where a highly decentralized approach has led to duplication of effort, the problem does not necessarily have to be solved overnight and at great expense. Often, the integration of different systems is desirable, but the effort needed for conversion enormous. In these circumstances, it is better to pursue a strategy of migration between old and new systems rather than one of sweeping overnight change.

One machinery manufacturer, for example, had a number of customer databases: one was in sales; another had been set up by the service department; and a third was used by marketing for direct mail campaigns. The databases had evolved in parallel, had completely different data structures, and knew identical customer companies by different addresses and acronyms. A simple technical merger was impossible. Although the company's first idea was to solve the whole problem once and for all by replacing the three old databases with a single integrated new one, it was soon evident that the effort needed for such integration would have been extremely high, and the benefit relatively low.

Instead, a new database was designed, considerably more powerful than the old ones, which encouraged the three different users to put all new data into it. This ensured that the three parallel systems would not live forever, and obviated the immense effort needed for a blow-by-blow data cleanup. Thus migration strategy made it possible to start up a new database at relatively low cost, with a view to converting the total system at a later date, when much of the data is already stored in it and the users have become accustomed to the new structure.

Machine concepts: Simplicity is just as important in machine concepts as it is in systems. Guaranteeing process reliability is much more important than speed. No one would dream, for example, of equipping an express parcel delivery fleet with Formula 1 racing cars. Although they lack trunk space, these vehicles would be able to get from point A to point B very fast. However, because of their extremely high-performance design, they would be much less reliable than a standard vehicle, so that average customer service levels would be lower.

Absurd as this example may appear, it describes precisely the phenomenon often found in mass-production facilities. High-performance machines with extremely high cutting speeds are installed, and then optimized still further to extract the last 10 or 20 percent of performance. These highly expensive machines are then fitted with highly complex tool change and automatic pallet change management systems to ensure that the machine, bought at considerable cost, will run all the time. To guarantee utilization, a special tool carrier is developed, which allows random machining of an enormous variety of parts.

This integrated system, undoubtedly a miracle of technology, is often so temperamental that the Formula 1 effect sets in. Although every individual decision in the upgrading process may have been plausible in principle, and served to get the optimum utilization out of a significant investment, the overall result is counterproductive. Companies that use such systems fail to follow the basic rule of simplifying the environment first and then solving the task with the simplest possible, controlled technologies.

FORGE AHEAD WITH SOME, EXPERIMENT WITH OTHERS

Despite the successful companies' much lower IT expenditure, they still use new machining technologies far more than the less successful companies. The successful companies stick to a simple principle. On the one hand, they invest heavily in those technologies whose controllability and benefits they fully understand. On the other hand, they are pioneers with untested new technology, but start with pilot applications, so that they can experiment with the technology's possibilities and limitations.

So, although the successful companies are ready to take risks with experimental technologies, when it comes to proven technologies they aim for targeted applications, oriented to clearly defined objectives.

Experimenting with Innovation

The successful companies try to understand the costs and benefits of new technologies early on, but do not tie themselves down with extensive investments straight away. They use CAD systems, for example, much sooner than other companies and are, in many cases, pioneers in the use of NC technologies.

Successful Western—not just German—machinery and component manufacturers do much the same in this respect as their successful Japanese counterparts. The Japanese invest heavily in pilot plants or installations, where they find out in precise detail what value and what expenditure they can expect. Western managers being shown around these pilot factories often come to the fallacious conclusion that the Japanese have much more automation than they do. They thus assume that their only chance of remaining competitive is to make bold major investments in new technologies.

In reality, the Japanese operate their normal production facilities more often with standard technologies than with leading-edge innovations. They do not introduce such technologies into their factories until they have learned how to control them in pilot applications, and are sure that they will help them to reach new breakpoints.

Successful Western machinery and component manufacturers do exactly the same. Since a full-sized pilot facility would account for a large share of their total production volume, they opt instead for pilot installations or applications too. Once they understand fully the costs and benefits, and have refined the systems, they invest systematically and heavily in manageable technologies.

Optimum time utilization plays an important role in the experimental

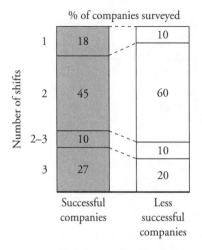
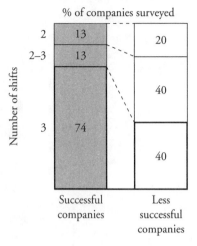

High hours of utilization are the primary concern with flexible manufacturing systems.

Exhibit 5-4. Utilization of Plant

phase, since investments at this stage are still often high and companies want to learn as much from them as possible. Flexible manufacturing systems (FMS) are the main technologies still used at this stage. Although they are no longer regarded as exotic, their value is not yet well enough understood for widespread introduction. To keep them within financial bounds and to gather as much experience as possible, German companies primarily operate them—unlike the rest of their machinery—in three shifts (Exhibit 5-4).

But this approach has its disadvantages. In a flow manufacturing system, operating a bottleneck machine in three shifts inevitably leads to an accumulation of stocks on both sides of it, which naturally interrupts the flow and adversely affects response times. In this respect, operating the machine in two shifts, to match general shift times, would make more sense, but would reduce machine productivity.

That situation does not worry the Japanese. In many cases, they have one-half to two-thirds of the machine productivity, but much higher labor productivity. Yet the capital cost of FMS is evidently so high that payback

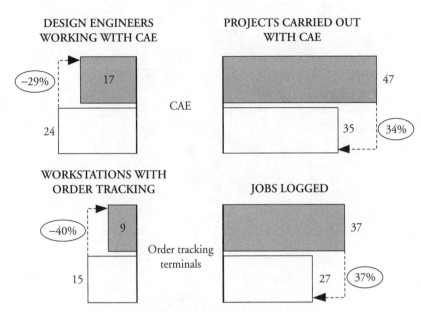

DESIGN ENGINEERS WORKING WITH CAE

-29%

17

24

CAE

PROJECTS CARRIED OUT WITH CAE

47

35 — 34%

WORKSTATIONS WITH ORDER TRACKING

-40%

9

15

Order tracking terminals

JOBS LOGGED

37

27 — 37%

In CAE and order-tracking terminals intensive technology utilization is the winning factor.

Exhibit 5-5. Machinery and Component Manufacturers: Spread and Utilization, 1989 (%)

seems feasible only with three-shift operation. The future penetration of FMS will depend largely on how far users can control the pressure toward flexibility that seems to be driving their installation, and how far FMS manufacturers succeed in achieving significant cost and price reductions by simplifying FMS concepts and tailoring them to these reduced requirements.

The current trend of operating FMS in three shifts, with the third shift often unmanned, or operated with reduced staff, is not a good model for proven technologies. This has certainly been the case with CAD systems. Technological progress and widespread installation have now reduced costs considerably. And the benefit is now so well understood that three-shift operation is no longer necessary, even to gain experience.

Forging Ahead with Proven Technologies

Some technologies, such as DNC, were experimented with early on by the successful companies and, in general, rejected as not generating enough

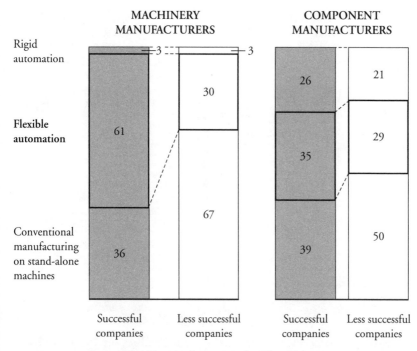

MACHINERY MANUFACTURERS | COMPONENT MANUFACTURERS

Rigid automation
Flexible automation
Conventional manufacturing on stand-alone machines

Machinery Manufacturers — Successful companies: 3, 61, 36. Less successful companies: 3, 30, 67.

Component Manufacturers — Successful companies: 26, 35, 39. Less successful companies: 21, 29, 50.

Successful companies | Less successful companies | Successful companies | Less successful companies

Successful companies have more flexible automation.

**Exhibit 5-6. Level of Automation, 1989
(% of number of production plants)**

benefit. If, however, a technology's benefit is significant and well understood, the successful companies will forge ahead with it whenever possible. But they still pursue a differentiated and highly targeted approach. Successful companies often invest less, but get more value than the less successful companies because they use the technologies more intensively.

The successful companies in Germany, for instance, have about 40 percent lower penetration of workplaces with order-tracking terminals than the less successful companies. But because they use the technology so intensively in those workplaces where it is installed, they still log almost 40 percent more jobs in absolute terms than the less successful companies (Exhibit 5-5).

All the successful companies, particularly the machinery manufacturers, have gone much further in flexible automation using CNC and CAD than the less successful companies (Exhibit 5-6). They have used the new

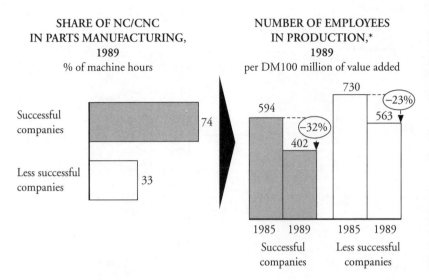

*Share of parts manufacturing approximately 50%

Greater use of NC increases the productivity lead of the successful machinery manufacturers.

Exhibit 5-7. NC/CNC Utilization and Production Productivity

technology primarily to automate previously conventional operations, rather than to bring flexibility to already rigidly automated machining operations. As a result, they have been able to realize potentials through automation that could not have been obtained with conventional approaches. This is one of the main ways in which the successful companies have further increased their already considerable productivity lead (Exhibit 5-7).

The successful CAD users do not indiscriminately pepper their engineering departments with CAD workstations. Quite the reverse. In contrast to the less successful companies, they know that the full benefit of CAD can be exploited only with appropriate standardization, and have thus created the necessary environment.

CAD systems are a good example of the underlying tendency toward early experimentation followed by heavy investment and then intensive use of the systems to a company's advantage. The successful machinery manufacturers started with the first CAD pilot applications in the mid-1980s. CAD penetration at that time was usually well under 20 percent,

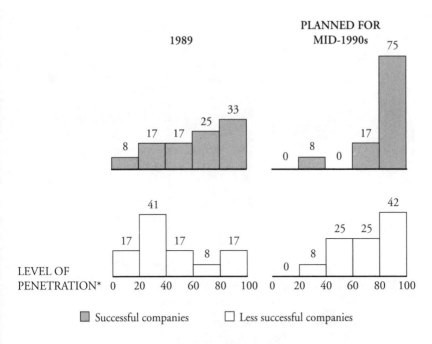

*% of staff working on CAD systems in development/design engineering

Successful machinery manufacturers companies have a five-year lead in CAD penetration.

Exhibit 5-8. Use of CAD in Mechanical Design (% of companies)

at successful and less successful companies alike. Over the next five years, however, the successful companies gained a much better understanding of the benefit of CAD systems and the best way to use them. And the gap in return opened accordingly when the roll-out came.

While six out of ten of the successful German companies now have more than 60 percent CAD penetration, only one in four of the less successful players has reached this level. It is also interesting to note that, of the successful German companies with a thorough grasp of the value of CAD technology, three-quarters are planning for almost 100 percent penetration by the mid-1990s, while less successful companies are trying to reach the successful companies' 1989 level by that time (Exhibit 5-8). The less successful companies thus have an application lag of about five years in a technology which is, in many cases, decisive for success.

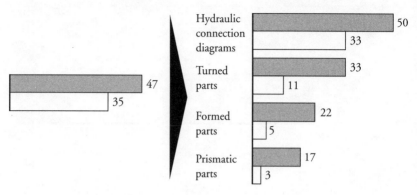

SHARE OF DESIGNERS WORKING ON CAD SYSTEMS, 1989

PRODUCTIVITY INCREASE FROM CAD

Hydraulic connection diagrams — 50 / 33

Turned parts — 33 / 11

Formed parts — 22 / 5

Prismatic parts — 17 / 3

47 / 35

■ Successful companies ☐ Less successful companies

Successful machinery manufacturers achieve higher productivity increases with higher CAD penetration.

Exhibit 5-9. Productivity Increases from CAD in Mechanical Design (%)

Their lead gives the successful companies a sustainable competitive advantage. Those companies with current CAD penetration of only 20 to 30 percent would find it impossible to speed up penetration at short notice, since training the team is a critical bottleneck factor, along with standardization. Attempting to increase the CAD usage of an entire department or division from 20 to 90 percent within two years would reduce the team's output for that period by about 40 percent. Moreover, it would not be sufficient to rely exclusively on exchange of experience among design engineers to provide training; the learning curve would inevitably be flat because almost the entire team would be CAD beginners.

It is for such reasons that the successful machinery manufacturers get far more benefit from introducing CAD. They achieve much greater productivity improvements in mechanical engineering design—not the most important indicator for successful CAD use, but one of the most comparable (Exhibit 5-9).

✦ ✦ ✦

EVEN WITH INTENSIVE USE, computer technologies may contribute little to increasing profit. This happens when they are grafted wholesale onto complex product concepts and structures. When, on the other hand, they are used to optimize simple, manageable tasks that also create real customer value, the potential can be considerable. Real improvements on the order of 30 percent lower cost, less time, and higher quality over a five-year period have been achieved.

The successful companies have not achieved such results by rushing into automation on all fronts, but by taking a highly selective and targeted approach:

+ Strategic concentration ensures that only those technologies are pushed whose value/benefit has previously been explored by detailed experimentation. Such experiments keep companies on the trail of the latest leading-edge technologies. For their ongoing operations they look for the simplest possible technologies, including standard machines and software, to ensure stable delivery capabilities and quality.

+ Internal and external interfaces are arranged by the successful companies in such a way as to minimize the need for coordination. They design their systems in a similar way, and reject theoretically achievable optimization in favor of strengthening their managers' entrepreneurship and scope of action.

+ In automation procedures they follow the law of simplicity. Before they introduce computer technologies, they rigorously simplify products, structures, systems, and machinery.

In our experience, creating the conditions for automation and getting technologies like CAD and CAM fully established in the right way can take three to five years. But significant progress can be made en route. The limiting factor is the speed not only at which the organization's functional attitude can be changed but also—and perhaps most important—at which the necessary skills can be spread throughout the team.

6

ORGANIZATION

✦ ✦ ✦ ✦ ✦ ✦ ✦ ✦ ✦ ✦ ✦ ✦

Transparency and Entrepreneurship

*L*ET us assume that your company's product range and customer base are now focused at your core; that close cooperation with selected suppliers helps you achieve the optimum level of vertical integration; that product development processes are designed to minimize risk upstream and ensure cross-functional integration; and that your plant locations have been selected to facilitate materials flows. Let us also assume that you have managed to sustain this happy state for some years. Then, according to our surveys and experience, your competitive position is unassailable and you are on an expansionary and highly profitable course.

The truth is that that is making a lot of assumptions, and few companies, either through past strategies or historical realities, achieve all of them. Indeed, even if they do achieve them, few operate in the cross-functional manner that is needed to tie them all together. Not surprisingly, few can bring them together in the form of an organizational environment that provides organizational transparency and strategic entrepreneurship.

In the past few years considerable thought has been given—around the world—to how to organize for sustainable competitive advantage. Much of this thinking grew out of the realization that traditional organizational theory, with its focus on sophisticated, tailored structures, was not preventing decision-making processes from taking too long or getting the wrong answers, nor administration from becoming an almost fanatical end in itself. At the same time, many companies with what organizational theory would consider untidy structures seemed to be thriving. In recent years, organizational theorists have begun to point to a company's dominant corporate culture as the key to improved decision making.

In the meantime, current trends continue to drive the change. In Germany, companies that over many years have developed "hard" organizational structures, with several layers, are now concerned about fostering autonomy and motivation. The command-and-control culture, they now believe, has to give way to organizational forms imbued with personal initiative and self-determination if they are to maintain the growth patterns of the past.

The basic validity of this value change has been borne out in our work with clients. Organization should not be seen primarily as a means to maintain order, but as a way to facilitate creativity and adaptability. Above all, the commitment of staff to corporate growth and innovation is without doubt the pivot of success. But as always there is skepticism in Germany— as elsewhere—especially among middle managers, about the course the change is taking. There appears to be a risk that companies will lose their clear sense of direction, and that—as happened with the overemphasis on structure—the vital ingredient of balance will be lost in diffuse efforts to please everyone.

The really successful companies appear to have resolved the dilemma. Once again, greater simplicity emerges as the leitmotif of their approach. This is expressed in unequivocal strategic signals from top management: proposing a clear vision, installing the right structures and procedures, and energizing staff. These signals, in turn, are translated equally unequivocally into practical requirements at the operational level:

+ For vision: accepted, simple goals.

+ For structures and procedures: self-managing, decentralized units.

+ For staff: competence, flexibility, and motivation.

Only when all three elements are directed toward the same end can they have a sustainable positive impact on competitiveness. Since they are closely interrelated, none of them can be changed without affecting the others. In ideal cases, this interaction and uniformly focused change generates a simple "cybernetic" system—a self-correcting, learning organization.

SIMPLE GOALS

Reducing the throughput time for a customer order from its receipt to the delivery of the finished components from 15 days to 1 day appears at first an ambitious goal. Once achieved, however, it becomes a powerful competitive weapon. But even with the inevitable ups and downs, something else will have been achieved that is at least equally important. The shared effort will have welded together a team that is capable of great achievements, with confidence in its ability to produce top performance, and highly motivated to repeat the experience.

The U.S. company Allen-Bradley underwent such a process some years ago. The company's experience is a textbook example both of what can be achieved by people who accept a shared goal and of what kinds of goals can generate this impact. They should be:

+ One-dimensional, to ensure that they are transparent and easily understood. The starting point (15 days from door to door) and the desired finishing point (completion within a day) could not be plainer.

+ Credible, because they come from a neutral source—i.e., one that is not biased in favor of any particular function. Coming from top management and driven by customer value, the objective could not be dismissed as irrelevant or unattainable. Moreover, it was positive, geared to market success, and easy for everyone to identify with.

+ Market- and customer-oriented. The short delivery time meant that OEMs, which normally carried the products of two component makers, were able to economize on warehousing because components no longer needed to be held in inventory.

+ Setting a general direction at the strategic level. The "15 to 1" goal left plenty of scope for the choice of problem-solving method.

+ Performance-related at the operational level, with practical targets.

Interim objectives were set for deadlines and functions—e.g., order processing, manufacturing, packing, and shipping—which helped keep all the participants on track at all times.

+ Uncoupled from other parameters, i.e., they expected no trade-offs, which not only confuse substance and accountability, but also complicate processes and systems.

Such objectives are the first and possibly the most important step toward a competitive edge in competence and motivation. This step is not always taken successfully. We all know of bold top-management visions that have failed to filter through to operations or have been dismissed as "absolutely impossible." And we have all seen top management teams, swamped with day-to-day preoccupations, that have no time to set a strategic direction because they have to deal with every operational detail in order to be able to direct the necessary action. Neither of these approaches leads to the desired simple, realistic, universally understood goals accepted as a basis for action—or even to independence and initiative taking.

Above-average companies demonstrate time and time again, at both the strategic and the operational levels, the noble art of pursuing one-dimensional goals focused on real customer value—in cost, time, or quality—that allow improvement of other dimensions at the same time, and are readily measurable. They also know what to avoid at all costs: excessive detail that smothers all motivation to take initiatives, or excessively long planning horizons that produce more theory than practice.

One-dimensional goal: The most important one-dimensional goal for machinery manufacturers appears to be high labor productivity. Successful companies often achieve double the value added per employee of their less successful competitors. That this is sometimes at the expense of machine productivity is no oversight, but deliberate policy (Exhibit 6-1, Exhibit 6-2).

High labor productivity levels—double those of good European companies—are also one of the key factors behind the success of leading Japanese manufacturers. While Western companies often invest in advanced technologies that need cumbersome infrastructures (quality assurance,

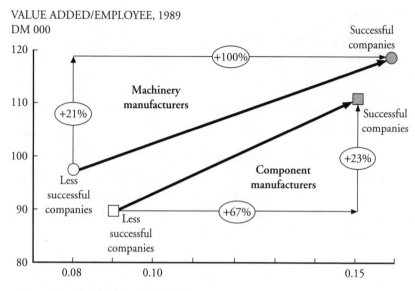

VALUE ADDED/EMPLOYEE, 1989
DM 000

Successful companies use high investment to foster labor productivity in particular.

Exhibit 6-1. Labor Productivity and Investment Ratio

materials management, maintenance, retooling mechanics, and machine operators), the Japanese concentrate on stabilizing production at a high level of scheduling, which allows them to reduce these infrastructures dramatically. It is not uncommon, for example, for Japanese companies to spend a lot of time ensuring that materials needed for production are available when they are needed—90 to 95 percent of the time. As a result, the capacity utilization of their factories is high compared with German— and even U.S.—companies, which have only 50 to 55 percent materials availability and consequently low capacity utilization. The team concept, which integrates all the necessary functions, and the lower product variety frequently found in Japanese companies are other valuable tools.

Neutral source: The ability to set general objectives from a neutral source, which does not favor any particular function, clearly distinguishes the suc-

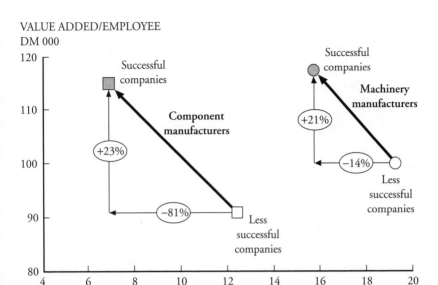

VALUE ADDED/EMPLOYEE
DM 000

The successful companies place less emphasis on machine productivity.
Exhibit 6-2. Labor and Machine Productivity, 1989

cessful from the less successful companies in the machinery and component manufacturing industries we studied. For example, the successful companies set roughly quantified vertical integration targets—mainly by defining the core areas where technological differentiation is desired—and leave the details to the decentralized divisions and departments. The less successful companies, on the other hand, often prescribe highly detailed cost-reduction objectives, together with individual make-or-buy decisions, for individual functions.

It is not uncommon, however, for the neutral top management at successful companies to take make-or-buy decisions, for example, that affect the entire company or are deemed strategic; at less successful companies these decisions are taken individually by the divisions affected.

Similar levels of detail apply to production planning and control: successful companies are satisfied with outline planning for parts manufacturing—that is, with a time horizon of approximately 80 to 90 days, which, in manufacturing, is a time horizon over which deadlines have a good chance of being met. The less successful companies try to make detailed plans for 150 to 200 days—resulting in production schedules fraught with modifications.

In the United States, we found companies with a planning horizon of 60 to 90 days. A 60-day horizon would appear to be somewhat short, especially in light of the longer throughput times we saw in these companies.

Decouple trade-offs: The successful companies also decouple trade-offs, so that employees are not trying to optimize so many variables at the same time that the process begins to resemble a death spiral. The parts-manufacturing function of one Japanese machine tool builder is an extreme example of such decoupling. No guidelines exist for determining optimum lot size in this company. When we asked about the reason for what would be considered in most operations management a grave sin of omission, we were told:

1. The company president was too old to understand the complicated optimum lot-size calculations.

2. The university graduates on the staff try to work out the optimum lot size for several thousand parts and hundreds of machines, with complicated methods like the Andler lot-size formula. However, their efforts almost invariably end up in an unproductive debate on the machines, parts, and cost elements to be included in the calculations. Moreover, the highly complicated models they produce can be interpreted one way or another, depending on one's point of view—a process that rarely leads to optimization.

3. Motivation of employees is difficult with lot size optimization. Let us assume that an optimization model shows that the lot size is too big. If it is reduced, the cost of inventory falls, but setup costs rise. That dilemma can be solved only with very complex mathematics, and even then, the formula works only for part A on machine B at time C. So

COST

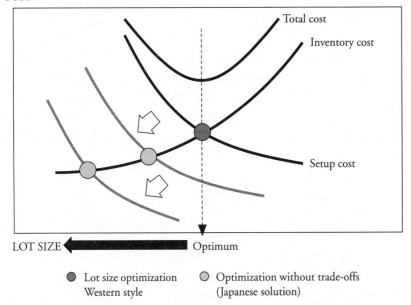

Total cost

Inventory cost

Setup cost

LOT SIZE ⬅ Optimum

⬤ Lot size optimization ◯ Optimization without trade-offs
  Western style (Japanese solution)

The Japanese avoid the time- and resource-consuming search for the optimum lot size by uncoupling the problem.

Exhibit 6-3. Western and Japanese Optimization Approaches

the company decoupled the two areas and made one person responsible for setup costs and another for inventory costs. If, for example, new technology and procedures reduce setup costs, they automatically move toward very small lots. Or if setup time is only minutes, optimum lot size is no longer a problem. So both managers are motivated by their mutual success instead of constantly arguing about the right lot size.

In addition, by decoupling the trade-off, the firm was no longer optimizing within existing targets, but challenging the targets. Because no trade-off was required, simple, achievable objectives could be set. Indeed, not only did the company not waste time figuring out the intersection of fixed setup cost and inventory cost curves, it shifted both curves entirely (Exhibit 6-3). Many German companies are now beginning to realize that more can be achieved for flexible manufacturing and lot size optimization with this "decoupled" approach than with the most sophisticated concepts and massive systems support.

One result of decoupling: when Japanese automotive manufacturers developed retooling technologies and procedures for large pressing lines, they proved the same point. It is now the norm to retool in less than five minutes with 1,000-tonne large-scale presses. In annual competitions or at the peak performance of individual pressing shops, the record times are less than three minutes. In Western companies, the procedure often takes about 20 minutes.

The difference, a decisive one for management by simple, realistic objectives, affects the entire work culture. German companies' corporate departments, for example, are often exclusively preoccupied with structure, determining who does what to the point of detailed job descriptions. In Japan, most of the effort goes into describing the organization's objectives. In an interview, one Japanese manager described the difference by the following analogy: "You Germans are organized like crayfish. Your hard shell, in which you take great pride, may give you a clearly defined exterior, but it also inhibits you. Our organization is more like a jellyfish. Naturally, it too has an outer skin that marks out our boundaries with the world around; but it is flexible and continually adapts to new requirements and conditions."

This manager was under the impression, rightly so, that Germans normally place more emphasis on delineating exact boundaries between organizational units: where the decision-making competence of an individual starts and finishes is precisely defined, right down to operational rules about what an employee should and should not do in specific cases. In Japan, only the definition of the "center" or of the objectives for one's own organizational unit is important; demarcation with other units is flexible and can be altered and re-altered to fit the situation. What a unit has to achieve within a certain period is laid down, but the way and the means remain open. Since these units are subsequently measured by their goal achievement, and are often actually in competition with other divisions from other production facilities, a transparent, constructive performance-based culture is created. For German companies today it is important to ensure that organizational structure does not stifle entrepreneurship and motivation at all levels.

SELF-MANAGING, DECENTRALIZED UNITS

One of the primary ways in which German companies support and encourage entrepreneurial spirit is in the design of their organizational structures and procedures. The buzzwords of entrepreneurship are equally common at both the successful and the less successful companies. But whereas the less successful companies only pay them lip service, the successful companies ensure that the words are backed up with implementation. That goes for all the popular phrases, from "market and customer orientation" and "cost-benefit responsibility" through "delegation." They are all implemented through self-managing, decentralized units.

Market and Customer Orientation

Although most of the less successful machinery and component manufacturers have functional structures, some 70 percent of the successful companies are organized by products or product groups. Anything else, they say, breeds bureaucracy rather than entrepreneurship. Accordingly, only 23 percent of the successful companies are organized by functions, and very few adhere to more complicated structures, such as matrix organization (Exhibit 6-4).

The same general picture also holds true in the United States, although there the functionally organized company is still quite common. Thirty-nine percent of the successful U.S. companies we surveyed (compared to 8 percent of less successful companies) are organized by product, 22 percent in a matrix (compared to 29 percent), and 39 percent by functions (compared to 63 percent).

These companies' manageably sized units are formed on the basis of different criteria, mainly determined by breadth of product range. Single-product companies, for example, primarily tailor their organizational units to strengthening those core processes that can have a direct impact on profitability. They set up such units or project teams as "order processing,"

TOTAL COMPANY STRUCTURED BY

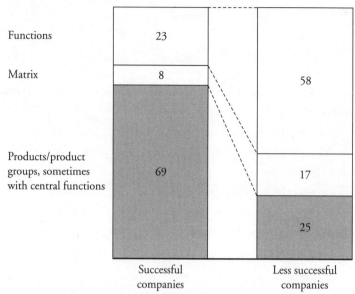

Successful companies are organized by products, not function.

Exhibit 6-4. Organizational Forms at the Top Level (% of mentions)

responsible for overseeing customer orders from door to door, or "product development," covering not only product specification and full-scale production, but every activity in between. In Germany, the "supplier management" core process could have a particularly high potential, whereas in the United States, concentration of suppliers is already common practice.

In multiproduct companies in Germany, particularly when the individual products or segments have different market requirements, units are organized around products. This orientation is a particular characteristic of the successful companies. One principle is widely established: products or services provided in-house that are also available on the open market—and for which, therefore, a market price exists—must prove their value against that market. On that basis, every organizational unit must do business with suppliers and customers as a profit center, and stay competitive with alternative sources of supply. Where there is no true external market, cost-center organization is preferred, as an even simpler solution.

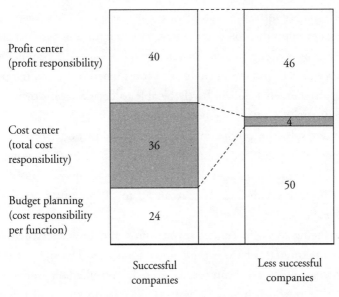

	Successful companies	Less successful companies
Profit center (profit responsibility)	40	46
Cost center (total cost responsibility)	36	4
Budget planning (cost responsibility per function)	24	50

Successful companies manage production facilities as cost centers.

Exhibit 6-5. Control of Production Facilities (% of mentions)

According to our studies, profit- and cost-center structures are well established at eight out of ten of the successful machinery and component manufacturers in Germany. Cost-center organization is not very common among the less successful companies, which tend to organize by functions, controlled through set budgets (Exhibit 6-5).

The same analyses in the United States showed that 50 percent of the successful companies have installed profit centers, compared to only 15 percent of the less successful companies.

Cost/Benefit Responsibility

Analysis of a production manager's impact on the price/benefit ratio of his end products in a functionally structured organization reveals that he can have very little influence on a product's design—and, by extension, its manufacturability. Purchasing, which typically accounts for a major portion of cost (materials account for 50 percent of costs in German manufacturing industries), is similarly way beyond his sphere of influence. Nor can he influence infrastructure activities, such as quality assurance, maintenance, or even production planning, to achieve optimum cost/benefit. His own decision-making powers do not extend beyond the productivity of direct personnel. And even here he is so constrained by the central personnel department, that he will barely be able to decide on his own how far his productivity targets have been achieved.

As a result, the production manager in a functional organizational structure cannot influence more than 15 to 25 percent of manufacturing costs. If, by contrast, his unit is organized as a self-managing profit center, he can bring his influence to bear on 70 to 80 percent of the product cost/benefit.

Changing to profit centers involves first and foremost redefining all roles at the interfaces between individual functions. The right of the new "manufacturing" profit-center managers to be consulted on product design means that they can influence both product complexity and number of parts. This is bound to foster design-to-cost of components and subsystems. Moreover, it will be in the very personal interest of the profit-center manager to collaborate with purchasing to arrive at optimal make-or-buy decisions, in order to achieve a cost structure that will result in superior cost/benefit ratios.

Integrating suppliers and optimizing logistics procedures are also beyond the reach of the production manager in a functional system. The centrally controlled infrastructures with which he must deal are too inflexible and opaque for that to happen. With a change to a product-oriented profit center, these internal resources—such as quality assurance, materials management, or maintenance—come at least partially under decentralized responsibility. In such a setup, strategic orientation and customer-oriented performance become much simpler.

The Japanese use the term "critical operational responsibility" for this change. The basic idea behind the critical operational units is that, in procedures that are critical to corporate success, no interfaces are allowed that will prevent or hamper overall optimization. If these units are properly designed, a uniformity is achieved that facilitates optimization of the cost/benefit ratio over the total process, from customer order to final delivery.

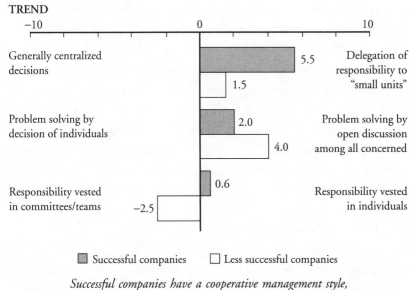

TREND

| −10 | 0 | 10 |

Generally centralized decisions — 5.5 — Delegation of responsibility to "small units"

1.5

Problem solving by decision of individuals — 2.0 — Problem solving by open discussion among all concerned

4.0

Responsibility vested in committees/teams — 0.6 / −2.5 — Responsibility vested in individuals

▨ Successful companies   ☐ Less successful companies

Successful companies have a cooperative management style, but with individual responsibility.

Exhibit 6-6. Description of Management Styles (scalar rankings)

Delegation of Responsibility

Uniform, basically self-managing units are a big step forward in themselves. However, the total potential impact will be much reduced if they remain structures only, without real entrepreneurship at all levels. In order to get the boxes in the organizational chart and the formal roles operating properly, the right procedures have to be installed. Responsibility and accountability must be established at the point where the greatest contribution can be made. Although this may seem axiomatic, experience shows that it bears repeating.

The trend toward solving problems through open discussion among all concerned seems to be increasing almost everywhere—in Germany as well as in the United States. Decision-making competence, on the other hand, is still often poorly organized. The successful companies delegate responsibility to decentralized units and individuals, while the less successful companies still emphasize central decision-making, primarily by jointly responsible teams or committees (Exhibit 6-6).

A revealing benchmark for how far responsibility is delegated is the upper limit for investment decision authority at different hierarchical levels. Top managers at successful German companies are often empowered to decide on sums twice as high as their colleagues in less successful companies. Moreover, at the less successful companies, four or five signatures are often needed for approval. At the second level of management, the gap becomes still more pronounced. Whereas executives at successful companies in Germany have investment limits of DM800,000 on average, their counterparts at less successful companies only have decision authority for sums up to DM160,000. We found the same kind of gap at the same management level in the United States, although it was less pronounced: a $1.3 million authorization limit for the successful companies, compared with $450,000 for the less successful.

The successful machinery manufacturers also owe their shorter throughput times, and therefore lower inventories in manufacturing, largely to the fact that they are more prepared to delegate responsibility. By adhering strictly to the planned work sequence, they reduce their working stocks to a minimum: 15 days in the manufacturing section, for example, 6 days at the machine groups, and 2 days at machine level. These top figures are due entirely to the German practice of putting control in the hands of *Meisters*. Detailed planning is left to the shop floor manager, who plans and executes how working stocks will be dealt with on site. The less successful German machinery manufacturers still plan and control 80 percent of their manufacturing centrally. These companies' working stocks are 22 days at machine level, 30 days at the machine group or shop floor management level, and as much as 44 days in the manufacturing section.

Similar, rather less dramatic differences are displayed by the component manufacturers. Here, however, delegation works the other way round. With their more stable processes and larger lot sizes, component manufacturers can successfully leave every detail to central production control or the manufacturing function.

Exactly how centralized or decentralized responsibility and competence need to be depends on the individual situation. Central systems can be used for the relatively straightforward planning and control of stable processes with little variation and large volumes. As processes become more complex and cumbersome, however, and the number of disruptive and other influencing factors to be taken into consideration rises, decentralized solutions will be more appropriate. The associated short feedback loops enable the decision maker to recognize problems immediately and take swift direct action.

The key factor here is to break down the overall rough strategic objective into concrete operational goals for all levels—down to the *Meister* or machine level in the manufacturing function, for example. Management on site is feasible if these goals meet the criteria described earlier in this chapter: that they are easy to understand, simple, and clearly relevant to market success; also, that employees are empowered to achieve them.

Most people are familiar, from visits to Japanese manufacturing facilities, with notice boards that continuously display plan-versus-actual comparisons of the unit production of a manufacturing section, or the utilization level or setup costs of a machine. Displaying annual targets against actual status is a constant reminder of the need for continuous improvement; and meeting such a requirement is the basis for compensation. If a company succeeds in mobilizing target consciousness and personal commitment at every level, a "performance-based culture" will develop, which in itself is a competitive advantage.

Our survey suggests that the proper allocation of tasks and accountability is more important in the introduction of computer-aided systems, for example, than the choice of a sophisticated technology. The successful German machinery manufacturers invest less than half as much in IT hardware and software (as a percentage of value added) as the less successful companies. Yet their labor productivity in administration is twice as high: they need 63 employees per DM100 million of value added, compared to 133 at the less successful companies.

One of the main reasons for the successful companies' efficiency lead is probably their strong emphasis on divisional and departmental responsibility. They put responsibility for the costs and success of IT projects directly in the hands of the user department. As a result, better tailored solutions are developed in less time, using fewer resources—and the person responsible for the project has a direct personal interest in actually realizing the potential benefits. Less successful companies, on the other hand, prefer standardized—and centrally controlled—project execution. Their success is correspondingly restricted.

COMPETENCE, FLEXIBILITY, MOTIVATION

Despite some fashionable assertions to the contrary, people are not the sole factor in corporate success. Yet without people or, more precisely, without their committed contribution, the rest would be worthless. Self-managing units with decentralized responsibility, for example, are a sound basis for achieving ambitious objectives and improving competitiveness. But getting them to work in practice depends entirely on outstanding competence and flexibility, delivered by a highly motivated workforce.

Competence and flexibility are really the only strategic competitive advantages available in many industries. Unlike product or service offerings, which can be imitated quite quickly, these qualities take some time to build and foster. At the same time, however, competence and motivation are not permanent fixtures. It can be very dangerous for a company to cling to a proven competence that guaranteed success in the past, but has long since become obsolete for competitive or technological reasons. That makes flexibility—and the motivation to change—all the more important.

Changes in Competence

The painful experience of the multibusiness conglomerates has demonstrated all too clearly that the marketing competence needed for market leadership in consumer goods is not the skill required for technology-based capital goods and vice versa. The key factor for success varies enormously by industry, too, whether it be time in consumer electronics, life cycle costs in investment goods, or product quality in components. However, the competence required changes over time as well, both over the life cycle of industries and also—and this is typically even less well understood—over the life cycle of individual products. The ability to recognize this in good time and to redirect corporate competence accordingly can have an enormous impact on whether a company succeeds or fails.

The change from mechanical engineering to electrical engineering to electronics to software in such areas as clocks and watches, measuring instruments, office equipment, and machine tools is a classic illustration of the dwindling value of once-dominant strengths. It can be seen both out in the market and internally—for example, in development departments, where the mechanical engineer has now been replaced by the physicist and the electronics engineer.

Looking at the life cycle of an individual product, the successful company will be the first one to both introduce a new technology and market its value to the customer at an acceptable price. Here, the key competence required is an in-depth knowledge of users and technology, together with their respective value profiles.

Once the new technology has been successfully launched, the battle for market position is on. If the business is seen as attractive and future-oriented, more and more companies will enter the market and supply may rapidly exceed demand. Even what starts out as quality-based competition inevitably becomes increasingly a cost/benefit struggle, and finally descends to pure cost competition. Only in the cost-based phase does it typically become clear which systems or standards will eventually dominate the market.

In this case, the core competence inevitably shifts from skills in technology introduction and technology leadership to the ability to develop global market shares and defend them in the long term. In other words, companies must be able to do more than just differentiate themselves technologically. They also need to be able to develop manufacturable products and design-to-cost skills, and be in a position to build worldwide sales and service networks. Failure in these competences will lead to loss of competitiveness in the volume segment. Once that has happened, only two options remain: going for a high-prestige, high-price niche, or quitting the market altogether.

The long battle to establish a single video system standard demonstrates the point. Despite their technical and qualitative superiority, Europe's Video 2000 system and Japan's Betamax system from Sony failed to catch on in competition with the VHS system, which was of no better than good quality, but much cheaper. The deciding factor was that VHS managed to take the lead with its software—the system rapidly achieved a dominant position in the video rental market.

Today, the Japanese VHS and Video 8 systems are battling it out for dominance in camcorders. Naturally, in the transition from one customer-value phase to the next, technical factors such as miniaturization, image and sound quality, and ease of handling play an important role. But competitive superiority in the—decisive—volume segment will depend largely on the ability to cut manufacturing costs to the bone.

Japanese competitors often assume that German—and even U.S.—industry lacks the ability to slash manufacturing costs, especially in areas where automation dictates cost. At a recent international discussion on the subject of factory automation in Japan, one Japanese participant advanced the argument that the acceptance of rapid automation in Germany is hampered by the belief in individual craftsmanship promoted by its *Meister* apprenticeship system. However, the Japanese participants recognized—and even admired—the level of mechanical engineering and precision engineering competence that the apprenticeship system in Germany has produced. But they had grave doubts as to whether the *Meisters,* with their focus on a single area of expertise, would actually be able to "master" the operational integration of electronics, data processing, and information systems that is required today to trim manufacturing costs. The Japanese seemed convinced that their training systems, which link mechanical and electronics competence, producing "mechatronic" engineers, were better.

Of course, it does not follow that the German apprenticeship system should be scrapped. But the training of the future will undoubtedly have to be designed and implemented in a more differentiated way if it is to meet changing needs. Every industry and every company will have to guard against optimizing skills and competences that are likely to be swiftly rendered obsolete by the current or future competitive environment.

The best of the machinery and component manufacturers in our study have largely succeeded in acquiring the necessary new technological skills. Their technically outstanding products bear witness to that. The problems they have had to overcome on the way should also give encouragement in what has now become an urgent need to achieve competitive cost structures.

The German machinery manufacturing industry plummeted by about 10 percent in world market share before reaching a precarious stability. In the early 1970s, the Japanese were adept at focusing on future-oriented segments, such as machining centers or lathes, and on key customer or geographic markets, such as the United States, and getting established in them with volume products nicely tailored to customer requirements. In addition, they managed to integrate mechanical engineering and electronics much faster than German competitors did. By the early 1980s, more than 50 percent of the machine tools produced by Japanese machinery makers were NC or CNC machines.

Today, thanks to their technology leadership, German machinery makers are still in a position to defend special segments and applications. But their cost disadvantages, some of them considerable, pose a threat that should not be underestimated. And the problem will become increasingly acute over time. The decisive question is: How fast can the German companies achieve the superior competence level of the Japanese—this time in manufacturing cost?

Significant progress has already been made in the sales and service functions of German machinery manufacturers. The successful companies have considerably stepped up their market coverage, despite drastic overall personnel reductions. They have almost doubled their number of sales and service staff per DM100 million of sales, while less successful manufacturers have retained their old structures. Companies that have invested chiefly in service—now a profitable business in itself—are now able to increase their unit sales in every region and segment. Companies compelled by necessity in recent years to play the specialist role are thus all set to earn good money in the volume segment.

Among component manufacturers the trend has gone the other way. The successful companies have reduced their marketing, service, and sales functions by about two-thirds over a five-year period. The leaders have primarily excelled at optimizing their service functions and central internal sales processing so as, ideally, to use the same systems, procedures, and processes as their customers. It is not unusual for this approach to boost productivity by 200 or 300 percent. The less successful companies are still working the market with their old-sized teams—and their productivity ratios have remained stubbornly below the old level.

Flexibility for Change

In an environment where new requirements call for constantly renewed competence, one traditional European strength—specialization to the point of perfection—will no longer be a sure-fire guarantee of success. In this respect, the Asians have something of a "natural" advantage.

One Japanese manager at a dinner illustrated this with the following analogy. "At a meal in Germany," he said, "there are three or four knives on the right, three or four forks on the left, and several spoons above the plate. A festive evening meal would be inconceivable without this array." In response to the argument that a well-laid table was a pleasant sight, and that such festive trappings added to the enjoyment, he replied, "All that is as it should be, but it is still typically German. For everything— even in a factory—you have special tools operated by specialist staff who are functionally organized.

"In Japan it is quite different," he continued. "You see, today we are eating with only two chopsticks, and we can handle everything with them from soup to the side dishes or fish and meat. What we use are simple tools, and we train our employees to have skills in the flexible use of these simple tools so that each of them can cope with every task."

The Japanese manager was only partly right. On a transfer line in Germany, for example, there are often five functionally separate teams of workers from manufacturing (machine operators, tool changers, and setup engineers), quality control, and maintenance. In Japan, there is often only one team, whose members can each perform all the functions or at least between them have all the necessary skills and competences. The exchange or integration of all necessary skills, coupled with a dialog-based management style, leads to high flexibility.

True, German training ideals lend themselves to an in-depth understanding of one special area rather than, for example, the cross-functional management know-how needed to optimize integrated procedures and functions. But specialization is not necessarily a constraint—if, for example, the learning skills included in specialist training can be applied as an independent strength elsewhere.

German machinery manufacturing has a pretty sound base in that respect. And the successful companies at least have evidently taken up the challenge. They are clearly less risk-averse, for example, than their less successful competitors when it comes to building know-how by employing specialists from other companies and from academia. Up to 50 percent of their top management are hired "from outside," compared to only 20 percent at less successful companies. The picture is similar at the second and third levels of management. (Naturally, the fast-growing companies can more easily afford to fill posts from outside, since they are not blocking internal careers by doing so.)

Almost 60 percent of the core personnel at successful machinery manufacturing companies in Germany are skilled staff; at the less successful, the figure is only 40 percent. And the successful companies in Germany invested over DM800 per employee per year in training over the period of the survey—almost four times as much as the industry laggards. (In the United States, this multiple was six times as much.)

It is at this point that the human factor really comes into play. Competence and flexibility can only be prescribed or taught to a limited degree. The urgently needed performance turnaround can only be realized with motivated staff.

Motivation to Change

Few issues are as controversial as the question of what motivates whom, or what makes someone motivate him- or herself. But there does appear to be a certain ranking in motivational factors. For example, up to a certain level, financial compensation plays a part, combined with a significant proportion of performance-related pay. Experience shows, however, that even top salaries will not permanently spur people on to peak achievement. Real, sustainable motivation can only be expected of highly skilled and knowledgeable employees, whose skills and knowledge are further developed by challenging tasks.

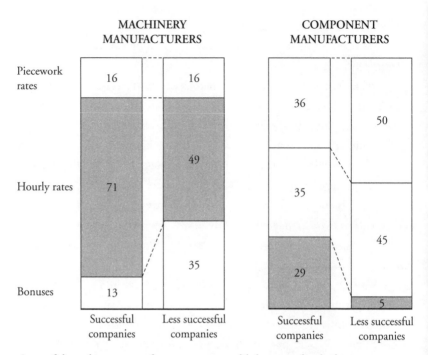

| | MACHINERY MANUFACTURERS | | COMPONENT MANUFACTURERS | |

Piecework rates: Machinery Successful 16, Less successful 16; Component Successful 36, Less successful 50

Hourly rates: Machinery Successful 71, Less successful 49; Component Successful 35, Less successful 45

Bonuses: Machinery Successful 13, Less successful 35; Component Successful 29, Less successful 5

| | Successful companies | Less successful companies | Successful companies | Less successful companies |

Successful machinery manufacturers are more likely to pay by the hour, component manufacturers more likely to pay bonuses.

Exhibit 6-7. Basis of Compensation for Wage Earners (% of staff)

Compensation systems: A striking feature of the compensation systems at German machinery manufacturers is the fact that flexible elements, such as performance-related bonuses, play a significant role only among sales personnel.

Our study did not reveal a uniform picture with regard to the importance of different forms of compensation. Of the two main forms of performance-related compensation—piecework rates and bonuses—piecework seems to have been retained only by the less successful German component manufacturers. Bonuses seem to have their primary motivating impact in companies that have simple, transparent procedures and manufacturing processes; they are little used at successful machinery makers and the less successful component manufacturers, but are well established at 30 percent of the successful component manufacturers (Exhibit 6-7).

In general, it seems likely that established compensation systems in

Germany are, to a certain extent, preventing companies from adapting to new requirements, such as introducing flexible working hours or the team concept. This makes it impossible to achieve the kind of continuous, incremental, step-by-step improvements which characterize the Japanese system and make it so successful. When piecework rates or bonuses can only be modified if there are major changes, for example, in the product, in manufacturing technology, or in procedures, it is difficult to introduce a performance-based culture fit to cope with the increasing demands of international competition.

Training: The rapid increase of in-house training is only partly a reflection of frustration at the inadequacy of the state education system. In-house training is designed to close skill gaps caused by changing requirements, and to encourage and motivate the high-school educated employee.

The absolute levels of spending mentioned above are not the only striking feature of in-house training. The successful companies are also distinguished by how they allocate the expenditure. While the less successful companies primarily invest in the top and second levels of management, the successful companies distribute their investment over the entire hierarchy, from top management to blue-collar employees (Exhibit 6-8).

Another feature characteristic of the successful companies is reminiscent of the Japanese mechatronic engineer's training. They train their staff not only to be functional specialists, but multiskilled experts who can master several functions and have broad management know-how. Job rotation, a notion without real substance at less successful companies, is normal routine at the successful German companies. In these companies, an average of almost one-quarter of the development team was previously employed in production. In quality assurance, just under 10 percent started in development, and 6 percent have transferred between quality control and production as a result of job rotation (Exhibit 6-9). In these companies, integration of functions and the exchange of specialist knowledge take place primarily through people, not through systems and complex processes.

While this is true for the companies in the German survey, we did not find significant evidence of job rotation in the United States. We

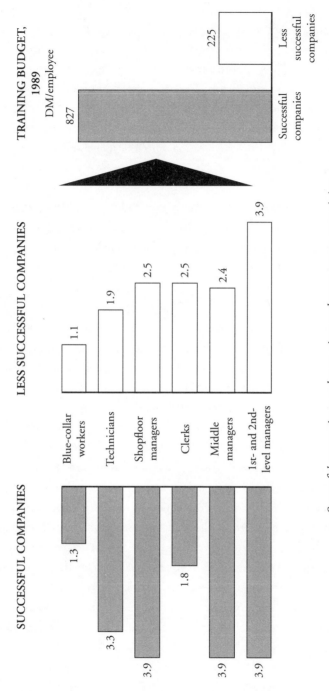

SUCCESSFUL COMPANIES

1.3
3.3
3.9
1.8
3.9
3.9

LESS SUCCESSFUL COMPANIES

Blue-collar workers — 1.1
Technicians — 1.9
Shopfloor managers — 2.5
Clerks — 2.5
Middle managers — 2.4
1st- and 2nd-level managers — 3.9

TRAINING BUDGET, 1989
DM/employee

827 — Successful companies
225 — Less successful companies

Successful companies spend more time and more money on training.

Exhibit 6-8. Training at Different Levels (days/worker)

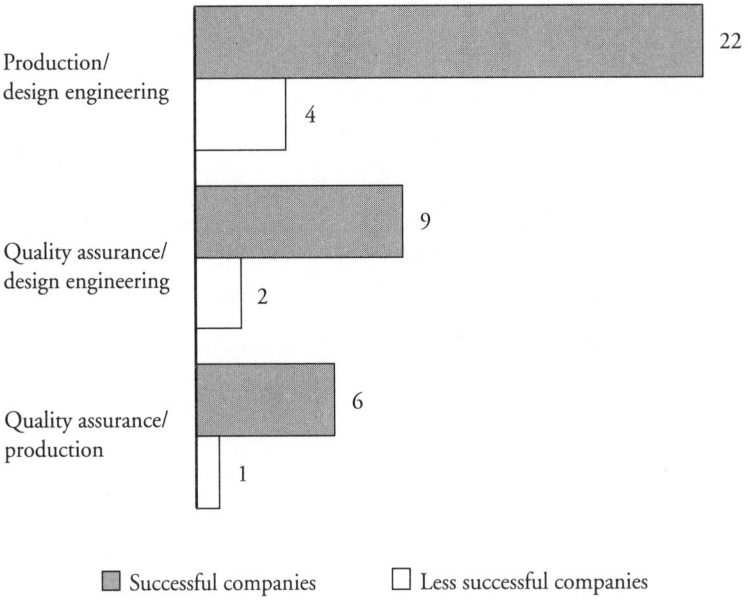
Production/
design engineering
22
4
Quality assurance/
design engineering
9
2
Quality assurance/
production
6
1
Successful companies
Less successful companies

More skilled workers in successful companies have experience in a variety of functions.

Exhibit 6-9. Transfer between Functions (% of total skilled workers)

believe there is still a high potential for improvement in this area for U.S. companies.

The skilling offensive seems to be well under way. If it is to help create and maintain a competitively superior organization, this offensive must now be pursued even more intensively and, above all, in an even more targeted way. But perhaps the greatest gap lies in communicating with staff and involving them in direction setting and decision making. The most important features here—completing the circle—are accepting and identifying with an ambitious but realistic goal that is "worth fighting for," achieving an appropriate level of autonomy and entrepreneurship, and setting up a partner-like dialog.

✦ ✦ ✦

IT IS HARD TO BE precise about the measurable competitive advantages of an organization that allows transparency and entrepreneurship to flourish. But the simplicity that enables the successful companies to achieve their outstanding strategic and operational performance would not be possible without such an organizational environment. Far harder to imitate than other strengths, organization itself will become an additional competitive factor—as the breeding ground of a performance-based culture and an independent driving force for targeted further development.

Where such an environment has become established, organization is not seen primarily as a structuring factor, but as an aid to the development of creativity, adaptability, and radical implementation:

✦ Strategic concentration orients the company to simple, broadly accepted objectives: achieving clear breakpoints in product and service offerings, and strengthening the most efficient stages in the value-added chain.

✦ Friction losses through interfaces are reduced to an unavoidable minimum because responsibility and the corresponding accountability are assigned to decentralized self-managing units. Externally, such units optimize their relationships with a small number of selected suppliers; internally, they ensure that core processes, such as order processing or product development, are not hindered by divisional boundaries.

✦ The procedures used by the successful companies get the best out of the well-designed "boxes in the organization chart." Far-reaching decision-making powers, delegation of responsibility, and continuous skilling—at all levels—secure competence, flexibility, and motivation. Together with partner-like dialog, they spark indispensable commitment to ambitious objectives that are worth fighting for.

To develop this culture, or to re-establish it where it has lapsed, often requires extreme pressure from outside or strong, visionary leadership from top management. Top management can implement this culture change—not by making grand statements or rallying employees to the flag, but by offering practical role models. Although this can often be achieved within six months or a year in small or medium-sized companies, large companies often need three to five years. If a performance-based culture cannot be created, a creeping loss of competitiveness is inevitable. This has been known to end in the bankruptcy of individual companies or the failure of entire industries.

7

FROM CONCEPT
TO PROGRAM

✦ ✦ ✦ ✦ ✦ ✦ ✦ ✦ ✦ ✦ ✦ ✦

Putting Simplicity into Practice

*T*HE simplicity that we have described has a positive impact on growth, liquidity, and return. This holds true in a variety of industries and countries. The factors that correlate most closely with the success of the machinery makers and component manufacturers we surveyed are summarized in Exhibit 7-1. They are all directly related to simplicity. Decentralized decision making, for example, is essential for simple procedures; a streamlined product range is simplicity's most visible expression; and higher value added per employee is perhaps the key outcome of reduced complexity.

Such simplicity ceased to be a natural condition a long time ago. The impulse to respond to complex problems with complex solutions has been too widespread and powerful. The six levers for fostering simplicity—product range and customer structure, vertical integration, concentration and integration of suppliers, development management, logistics, technology, and organization—therefore have to be applied deliberately. Their effectiveness, when applied with purpose, is what we have tried to describe and account for in the preceding chapters. Strategic concentration on a few, decisive parameters and simplicity in operations can both generate sustainable competitive advantages that have a measurable impact on corporate success.

In almost every case, the simplification process becomes a deep-rooted cultural transformation, a fundamental change program. This is often

DECREASING CORRELATION

MACHINERY MANUFACTURERS	COMPONENT MANUFACTURERS
• Value added per employee	• New hires from outside
• Streamlined product range	• Streamlined customer structure
• Total investment per employee	• Early definition of product specifications
• Low average employee age	• Share of single sourcing
• Job rotation	• Level of automation in production
• Share of single sourcing	• Low average employee age
• Share of superior products	• Total investment relative to value added
• Training investment	• Fixed-asset investment per employee
• Share of new locations (greenfield)	• Training investment
• Share of flexibly automated machinery	• Decentralized decision making

Exhibit 7-1. Most Important Contributions to Corporate Success

underestimated. And particularly widely underestimated is the importance of the interaction of organizational elements—vision and objectives, structures and procedures, energizing people—that are described in Chapter 6. It is not because the requirements at the organizational level are particularly complex. It is the reverse: the actions and interactions in question appear deceptively simple and are all too easy to dismiss as trivial, or to check off on the corporate "to do" list as long since accomplished.

But the differences in performance of comparable companies from the same industry—the gap between the successful and the less successful companies—leave no room for doubt. Appropriate management of the organizational environment is a powerful tool for corporate change. How well a company will cope with the major changes looming in the next five to ten years will depend on whether it can steer that change, rather than letting it take its own course.

It is never too soon to make a start. But, at the very latest, alarm bells should ring when loss of market share, declining profits despite rising sales, and long innovation or decision-making processes become apparent. Such symptoms should trigger implementation of the change program, which can be given added momentum through a rigorous audit of the company's position, a fundamental analysis of the causes of problems, and a practical process of simplification.

CHANGE PROGRAM: ORGANIZING THE TRANSFORMATION

The change program should (re)model the internal corporate environment in such a way as to trigger a process that will ensure continuous renewal and continuous learning. That can only be achieved through an integrated approach, but one that also takes into account the company's stage of organizational development.

In a functionally structured company, for example, where market orientation by products or core processes is not yet a characteristic of the organization, project teams with overall product responsibility should be set up as a first step. For an important product group, a cross-functional team should be appointed that will stimulate top management. The team will be responsible for analyzing the strategic position of its business, developing a profile of strengths and weaknesses, and setting ambitious market goals that are "worth fighting for." It will also have to determine what cost, time, and quality breakpoints have to be met and what core processes need to be optimized in order to achieve objectives.

If the groundwork is done properly, the company will gain more than some transitory, albeit useful, experience in project work. In the course of the change program, the often inward-looking functional orientation will give way to an outward-looking market focus. Cross-functional cooperation will be regarded as an enrichment and a support—and will be practiced accordingly. Increased product responsibility will become the test case, the model, or even the pioneer of new organizational forms in the company. Employees will find dormant skills awakening, will develop and—above all—will give their commitment.

An important prerequisite for all this is that the project team must be made up of people who possess not only the necessary technical skills, but also the potential for future managerial responsibility. The best are needed for the change program.

THE STARTING POINT:
A COMPARISON WITH BEST PRACTICE

As we have seen, the successful companies are not only outstanding in one of the dimensions of cost, time (= speed of response), or quality (= product value), but also rank well above the average in all three. To get a rough fix on a company's strategic position, all that is needed is to profile its strengths and weaknesses compared to those of the best competitors and against customer requirements in these categories.

Meaningful benchmarks are relatively easy to identify, for example:

+ Cost: One good indicator is labor productivity in terms of value added per employee—for the company as a whole and for the individual functions.

+ Speed: The ability to respond quickly to market changes in terms of innovation or delivery capability. This can be measured either by

STRATEGIC POSITION	AVERAGE	SUCCESSFUL*	LESS SUCCESSFUL*
Cost			
• Labor productivity (DM 000 value added/employee**)	103	119	99
Speed (highly product dependent)			
• Development time (months)	—	13	30
• Manufacturing throughput time (weeks)	11.9	7.8	15.6
Product value			
• Share of superior products (%)	47	64	26

*Average figures for group
**Annual increase approximately 5–8%

Exhibit 7-2. Checklist of Key Success Parameters, 1989: Machinery Manufacture

development time, from specification to full-scale production, or alternatively, by manufacturing throughput time.

✦ Product value: A lead in technology, product quality, and service. This can be measured, for example, by share of superior products in the target segment. Superiority can be measured by a weighted assessment against buying criteria.

Exhibit 7-2 give examples of comparative figures for the machinery companies from our German study. The column "Successful companies" shows averages for the group of successful companies. The absolute leaders among the participants tower above that figure. In labor productivity, for example, they made over DM200,000 of value added per employee in 1989; the increase since then is estimated at an average of between 5 and 8 percent per year. And an international comparison shows successful U.S. companies with up to twice the German "successful companies' average," and Japanese companies with three times.

The world's best competitor in the target segment, or better still the volume segment, should always be used as a benchmark. Benchmarking works particularly well in such comparisons. If a company already has a good deal of information about its own position, selected workshops with key managers may be enough to establish the gaps; if considerable uncertainties exist, a detailed strategic analysis is essential.

THE CAUSES OF PROBLEMS: GET RIGHT TO THE ROOTS

If the position audit has shown up weaknesses, a preliminary diagnostic scan can pinpoint performance gaps more accurately. This diagnostic should cover the parameters that correlate most closely with success or failure. Although it is no substitute for a detailed corporate analysis, a comparison with the figures for successful, average, and less successful companies will provide some clues as to sources of improvement potential.

Exhibit 7-3 gives an example of such a checklist, once again containing comparative figures drawn from the German study. The parameters, which differ slightly in importance and profile for the two different industries, relate to the most common reasons for performance gaps we found:

- ✦ Inadequate or misdirected investments, for example: investment per employee, investment in relation to value added, share of automated machinery, investment in new locations.

- ✦ Too much variety, overcomplexity, for example: number of products in relation to sales, level of customization, number of suppliers, number of customers.

- ✦ Low levels of competence, motivation, and flexibility, for example: age of staff, amount of job rotation, size of training budget, share of outside hires.

Applied to a company's real circumstances, this small selection of indicators provides an informative profile of strengths and weaknesses. They are a simple means of revealing where detailed analyses should begin.

CONSEQUENCES: SET THE FOCUS

There are many different ways of bringing about change and improving performance continuously, depending on a company's situation. The

CAUSES OF POOR PERFORMANCE	PARAMETER	MACHINERY MANUFACTURERS			COMPONENT MANUFACTURERS		
		Average	Successful	Less successful	Average	Successful	Less successful
Poor investment							
• Low total investment	• % of value added	12	22	10	13	18	8
• Low level of automation	• % of machinery	49	64	35	53	61	34
• Few new locations	• % of locations	26	50	12	28	33	17
High variety, overcomplexity							
• Product variety	• Number of products/DM100m sales	7	2	9	1,400	1,000	2,200
• High level of customization	• % of development capacity	13	12	16	—	—	—
• Supplier variety	• Number of suppliers/DM100m purchasing volume	1,200	300	1,500	1,300	1,200	1,800
• Little single sourcing	• % of purchasing volume	29	60	11	20	46	13
• Customer variety	• Number of customers/DM100m sales	—	—	—	300	25	500
Low competence, motivation and flexibility							
• Workforce too old (share of employees over 35)	• % employees	61	57	65	55	48	61
• Little job rotation (production/design engineering)	• % of staff in 5 years	7	9	6	17	41	2
• Small training budget	• DM/employee	490	980	260	240	300	180
• Few new hires from outside	• % executives p.a.	19	24	10	33	56	16

Exhibit 7-3. Checklist of Key Success Parameters, 1989

foundations for an assessment of the starting point, organizational skills, challenges, and opportunities are laid by the cross-functional project team's diagnostic and analysis of causes. The weaknesses identified here—or the need for improvement versus competitors and customer requirements—can be directly translated into action. This action will ultimately be aimed at reducing complexity and at simplifying structures, procedures, and interrelationships.

It is important to obey the commandment of simplicity in the simplification process, too. In other words, it is vital not to attack every issue at once with a variety of objectives, but to concentrate on one key lever. Depending on the results of the diagnostic, selecting and integrating a few core suppliers may have top priority, or it might be streamlining the product range, spinning off value-added stages, or realigning manufacturing to product-specific locations. The simultaneous further development of all other dimensions must be subordinated to the primary focus. And the change must be deliberately targeted to major change—the soothing, reassuring effect of marginal or incremental improvements must not be allowed to take root.

The process takes from one—in exceptional cases—to five years for the new procedures and structures to become a permanent part of the corporate culture. However, concrete improvements will start to take effect much sooner, and these will help maintain the necessary momentum.

Programs of this kind are not nine-day wonders. Successful ones lead to a continuous learning and adaptation process. All such programs and every fresh start have a small number of winning factors in common:

+ A simple, inspiring message conveying the overall objective.

+ Attractive goals, market-oriented and positive, which rapidly gain broad acceptance and for which it is worth making an effort.

+ The generation of increased autonomy through cross-functional teams with the right organizational environment.

+ The sense of "living" cultural change—from an internal to an external orientation, from "beating the competition" to "winning the customer," from "command-and-control" to "energizing the grass roots," from "100 projects of the day" to "key project of the year."

+ A pacemaker role and the visible commitment of top management.

+ Ongoing cross-functional communication at all levels.

That is the best and most direct route to sustainable competitive advantages in cost, time, and quality. Following this route will allow companies to eliminate complexity, open up creativity potentials, and achieve superior competence and motivation.

POSTSCRIPT

✦ ✦ ✦ ✦ ✦ ✦ ✦ ✦ ✦ ✦ ✦ ✦ ✦

A U.S. Comparison

*S*TANDORT *Deutschland!* (Locate in Germany!) In a gradually coalescing European Union, these words are a call to arms. Is it possible to manufacture competitively in Germany? With all the social benefits, higher wages and fringe rates, and dramatically shorter working hours enjoyed by German employees, why not move the plant to Spain? Why not move it to Turkey, or to one of the emerging economies of the recently liberated Eastern bloc? Indeed, why not move your manufacturing plant to the southern United States, where the sun is warm, the local governments stable and eager to please, and the labor-relations climate friendly?

Americans are flattered and pleased by the attention of European plant location specialists. They are also amused. It wasn't long ago that the same defeatist cries were heard in the United States. "Can America Compete?" journalists asked. Politicians tested the issue for voter appeal. Academics and professional economists testified about, wrote about, and studied the subject. The consensus was: "We'd better."

And so a lot of people set to work all over industrial America. TQM— total quality in everything we do. Kaizen—continuous improvement, step by tiny step doing your job a little better every day. Process reengineering—cutting out the paperwork, the needless duplication and lost time, the years of bureaucratic creep.

Germany—and behind Germany much of high-cost Europe—looks ahead to a long climb. Just because America started its climb a few years earlier does not mean it is necessarily ahead. The Europeans come from a different starting point, and are likely to follow a different course.

Just how different the challenge facing European manufacturing enterprises is from America's, this book makes clear. German companies operate in a world of niche markets, engineered differentiation, and embedded complexity. German engineering apparently has a dark side, a tendency toward the "not-invented-here" syndrome that surpasses even U.S. engineering, a professional thrill over the uniquely designed fastener, and a steadfast refusal to leave well enough alone. Apparently, few German general managers are aware of the golden rule of engineering management: "Sometimes it's necessary to shoot an engineer and ship a product."

But engineering is not the only function in Germany entangled in overpowering complexity, rigid rules, and calcified business practices. National marketing and sales organizations, one for each foreign country, help perpetuate nationally preferred product features, national functional specifications, and individualized terms of sale. However, the absence of well-established national distribution networks forces manufacturers to deal directly with thousands of small customers; handle logistics, installation, and service problems themselves; and administer mind-numbing paperwork.

Even the infrastructure conspires against simplicity. German labor unions, long ago cartelized by industry and often ensconced on the Supervisory Board (*Aufsichtsrat*), have made work rules and job standards matters of contract, so that even when companies invest in labor-saving equipment, they must negotiatiate with the union before job standards can be changed.

German industry must wrestle with enormous complexity—in its markets, in its supply base, and even within its own companies. As our survey and case examples make clear, simplicity is simply better. Fewer customers, fewer products, fewer suppliers, simpler and faster processes, and the organizational transparency that comes with homogeneous, self-managing business units are the observed formulas of the successful companies in Germany.

We carried out a survey similar to the one described in this book in the United States. We looked at 21 companies in the component manufacturing industry over the period 1987 to 1991. The findings from this survey, some of which are mentioned earlier, can be summarized as follows:

+ The U.S. business environment is much less complex than the German/European environment; at the same time it is more competitive and unforgiving.

+ In the United States, as in Germany, simplicity wins. America's most economically successful companies are relatively more simple in their customer and supply bases and in their internal management structures and processes than their less successful counterparts. However, in the United States the scales are shifted in favor of simplicity overall; America's least successful companies are about as complex as the most successful companies in the German sample. It follows, therefore, that the most successful U.S. companies are far simpler than their German counterparts.

+ In contrast to German firms, successful U.S. companies rely on labor productivity for their economic advantage. Neither low-cost labor, nor heavily capitalized automation, nor outsourcing to agile suppliers are part of the American success story. Successful U.S. manufacturers achieve twice the labor productivity of their German counterparts. And not coincidentally, they make twice as much money for their shareholders too.

MORE COMPETITIVE U.S. BUSINESS ENVIRONMENT

The U.S. survey results show wide disparities in profitability between manufacturing companies. In the same industry, enviably profitable, successful enterprises co-exist with lackluster firms, and gradually or rapidly shove aside declining and unprofitable competitors. This is true in growing and declining markets, in high- and low-technology product categories, and even in bad times in cyclical industries. Even in industries widely regarded

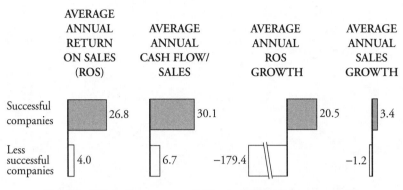

	AVERAGE ANNUAL RETURN ON SALES (ROS)	AVERAGE ANNUAL CASH FLOW/ SALES	AVERAGE ANNUAL ROS GROWTH	AVERAGE ANNUAL SALES GROWTH
Successful companies	26.8	30.1	20.5	3.4
Less successful companies	4.0	6.7 / −179.4		−1.2

Exhibit PS-1. Summary of Financial Performance (%)

as unattractive—stagnant or declining in overall volume, beset by over-capacity and cut-throat pricing, offering limited opportunities for competitive differentiation through technology or proprietary designs—highly profitable enterprises can be found.

For example, U.S. component manufacturing in the late 1980s and early 1990s was not popularly regarded as an attractive place to be. The customers of the component manufacturing companies, particularly the auto OEMs, were under immense cyclical profit pressure, and were still staggering from a decade-long loss of share to Far Eastern imports and transplant production. Sales volumes were not keeping up with inflation, as the OEMs called for price rollbacks to accompany ever improving quality and delivery performance.

Yet, despite this pressure, the top U.S. component makers did quite well economically. Their average ROS was an astounding 26.8 percent before tax. Cash flow/sales and average growth in ROS were also enviable. Only sales growth was lackluster, since—at 3.4 percent for the successful companies—it did not exceed inflation (Exhibit PS-1).

At least in comparison to its German counterpart, U.S. component manufacturing appears highly competitive. The most successful U.S. component manufacturers far outstrip their German counterparts in profitability. The less successful companies in the U.S., while on average over the period of the survey matching the performance of the less successful German companies, appear to be on a downward slope (Exhibit PS-2 and Exhibit PS-3).

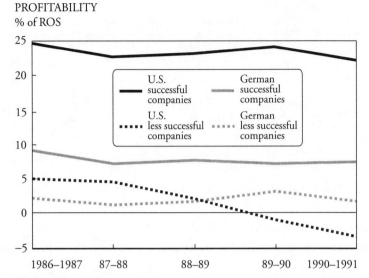

The U.S. appears to be a more competitive market for component manufacturers than Germany.

Exhibit PS-2. Comparison of U.S. and German Component Manufacturers

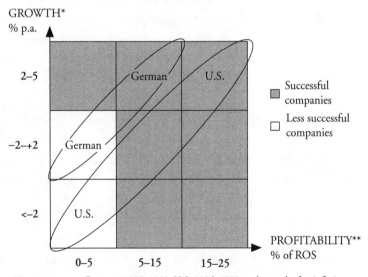

*5 years average, Germany 1985–1989, U.S. 1986–1990; real growth after inflation
**5 years average of EBIT/sales. If German pension reserves were added to EBIT, ROS would increase by 1–2 points

Successful U.S. companies outstrip their German counterparts in profitability.

Exhibit PS-3. Comparison of U.S. and German Component Manufacturers: 1986–1991

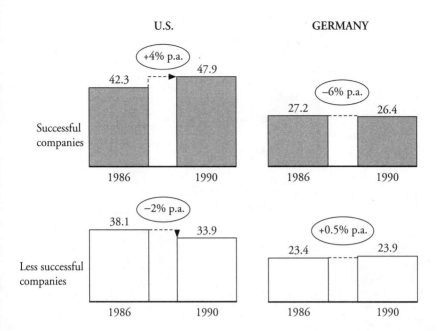

Note: Conversion on base of purchasing power parity (PPP) rates, inflation adjusted

Underlying the higher U.S. profitability is an increasing differentiation in labor productivity.

Exhibit PS-4. U.S.$ Value Added per Labor Hour of Component Manufacturers

Underlying the wide gaps in profitability between U.S. and German enterprises in the same industry are several dynamic factors:

◆ Principally, the United States appears to be a much more price-competitive market, which has driven U.S. managements to focus on costs, especially labor productivity. In the same industry—component manufacturing—U.S. workers add 60 to 80 percent more value per hour worked, and work 15 to 20 percent more hours per year as well (Exhibit PS-4).

◆ A major barrier to productivity improvement efforts in Germany appears to be the piece rate system, which effectively locks standard times into the labor contract. U.S. component manufacturers, in contrast, pay for less time as productivity improves, and indeed a surpris-

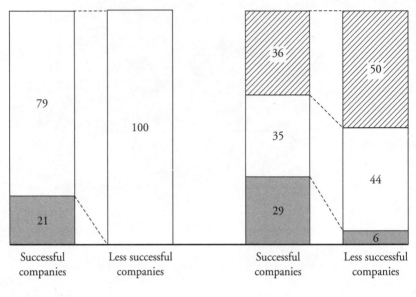

☒ Piece work   ☐ Time work   ▨ Bonus

In Germany, compensation based on piece work may be a hurdle to continuous improvement.

Exhibit PS-5. Compensation System for Blue-Collar Workers in Component Manufacturers (% of wage earned)

ing 20+ percent of successful U.S. component makers have found ways to share productivity improvements with blue-collar workers through group incentive bonuses (Exhibit PS-5).

✦ In Germany, product design appears to have been the major competitive drive for component manufacturers in the late 1980s and early 1990s; they did more customer-specific engineering, brought product development times down to two years (compared to four years in the United States), and spent almost twice as much on R&D (Exhibit PS-6).

These astounding differences in labor productivity among companies involved in the production of a similar market basket of goods stem, we believe, from the essential isolation of German component supply bases

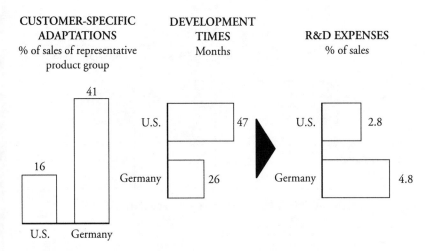

CUSTOMER-SPECIFIC
ADAPTATIONS
% of sales of representative
product group

41

16

U.S.   Germany

DEVELOPMENT
TIMES
Months

U.S.   47

Germany   26

R&D EXPENSES
% of sales

U.S.   2.8

Germany   4.8

In Germany, the competitive focus is much stronger on product design.
Exhibit PS-6. Component Manufacturers

from pan-European and especially global competition prior to about 1988. German assembly companies bought German parts, preferably from suppliers within a few hundred miles of their plants. As a result, the brutal forces of global competition were excluded—for a while—and a modestly profitable, highly complex, and essentially fragile component supply industry was encouraged to develop behind barriers of national business affiliation.

IN THE UNITED STATES AS WELL, SIMPLICITY WINS

As in Germany, the economically more successful companies in the United States managed to simplify their business challenge. They greatly streamlined their product lines to serve their customers with relatively fewer products (Exhibit PS-7).

Unlike their counterparts in Germany, successful U.S. component manufacturers have integrated their supply chain, both upstream and downstream. They buy a lower proportion of their value added from suppliers; they make rather than buy. They have many fewer suppliers and work with them much more closely than their less successful counterparts, in design, quality, cost, and delivery. Looking downstream to their custom-

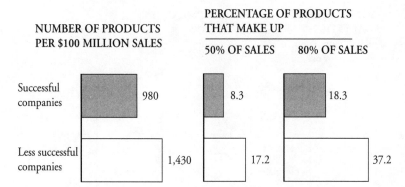

Exhibit PS-7. U.S. Product Concentration, 1991

ers, successful component manufacturers manage the whipsaw of volume and mix changes much better than their weaker competitors. In design, production planning and scheduling, and process layout, they remove the root causes of instability which draws factory floor people into fire-fighting and crisis modes.

It is instability, rather than complexity per se, that successful U.S. manufacturers seek to avoid. Thus we did not find, as our German colleagues did, that successful component manufacturers were de-integrating. On the contrary, successful U.S. component makers bring relatively more of their value added in-house, both because their superior productivity favors make over buy, and because higher levels of integration make the challenge of production volume and mix changes more manageable.

Internal simplicity is also a hallmark of successful U.S. companies. For example, successful U.S. component makers design components with a high degree of modularity to promote production stability. They have about as many piece parts to manage as their less successful competitors, but far fewer components and subassemblies, and about half as many finished products. They meet a greater proportion of customer demand with a few top-selling items, and cover most of the remainder of customer requirements with "pre-engineered specials"—products tailored to custom applications but assembled from predesigned modules rather than designed from scratch. As a result, their production flow is faster, smoother, and

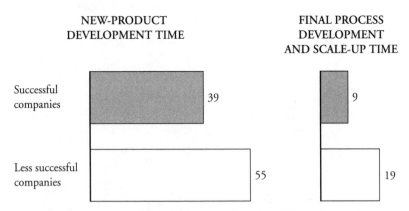

	NEW-PRODUCT DEVELOPMENT TIME	FINAL PROCESS DEVELOPMENT AND SCALE-UP TIME
Successful companies	39	9
Less successful companies	55	19

Exhibit PS-8. New-Product Development Time (Months)

less beset with late-stage engineering change notices (ECNs), leaving management more time to focus on productivity.

However, we did not find that there was much difference in the spread of the design function between the successful and less successful companies—in contrast to German manufacturers. The successful U.S. companies enjoyed a 10-month shorter new-product commercialization cycle, but their advantage comes almost entirely in the process design and ramp up of manufacturing volumes (Exhibit PS-8). Shorter design cycles, and commensurately lower design costs, do not appear to be a key factor for success in U.S. component manufacturing.

Rather, it is their ability to be market-driven, to reflect specific customer requirements in product design and manufacturing flexibility, that distinguishes successful U.S. component makers. Successful U.S. companies focus clearly on their customers' needs, measure customer satisfaction, and excel at tailoring their business systems to customers' requirements. One surprising result of this market focus is that successful U.S. component makers spend more as a percentage of sales on marketing and new-product development than their less successful counterparts (Exhibit PS-9).

This is in contrast to the German pattern, where successful companies spend less on both marketing and R&D than the less successful companies. Interestingly, however, successful companies in both Germany and the

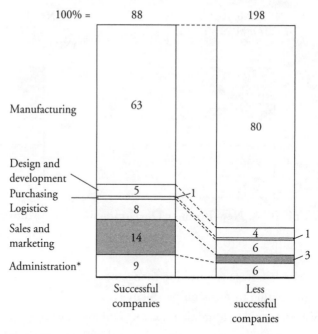

| | 88 | 198 |
| 100% = | | |

Manufacturing — 63 / 80

Design and development
Purchasing — 5 / 1
Logistics — 8

Sales and marketing — 14 / 4, 1

Administration* — 9 / 6, 6, 3

Successful companies

Less successful companies

*Includes Other category

Exhibit PS-9. Employees per $10 Million Added Value, 1991

United States spend approximately the same on these two functional activities as a percentage of sales, as nearly as differences in terminology and accounting practices allow us to determine.

MAJOR DIFFERENCE: IN THE UNITED STATES, LABOR PRODUCTIVITY IS KEY

In the United States, successful component manufacturers drive for labor productivity, rather than chase low-cost labor. Much to our surprise, we could find no statistical correlation between low labor rates and overall company profitability or growth. Instead, we found successful companies achieved double or better the factory workforce productivity of their less successful counterparts, and almost four times the net value creation (value added less labor costs) per employee. JIT, TQM, PDCA, MRPII, and a host of other productivity-enhancing tools and management approaches were applied by companies at both ends of our success spectrum. The differentiating factor appears to be that the successful component makers approach any tool with a results-oriented drive for productivity, whereas their less successful counterparts often appear to install the tools for their own sake.

As many other observers have found, successful U.S. managements empower factory floor teams to manage themselves. In successful U.S. component manufacturers real production decisions—what to make, what to accept or reject, how to break bottlenecks and solve problems—are driven down to the front-line team. Successful companies actually spend less on training and pre-packaged workforce-involvement approaches, choosing instead to give front-line workers more control over the important decisions that affect the workforce, and supplying them with the capital and decision-making influence to fix the problems that arise.

In contrast to other studies, however, ours did not find that higher capital intensity or superior automation played much of a role in strong U.S. labor productivity. Superior U.S. component makers squeeze twice as much out of capital. Capital spending rates correlated negatively with workforce productivity in our sample of U.S. component makers in the late 1980s and early 1990s.

During this period a number of companies—primarily in the less successful half of our sample—were in a catch-up mode, and were pouring money into new fabrication equipment after years of underspending and neglect.

In the successful top one-third of our sample, however, we found much better process understanding, closer control of capital spending overall, and a minimalist approach to capital investment. We believe that this approach is no mere cyclical phenomenon, but an intrinsic and permanent characteristic of the successful companies' behavior. Interestingly, we found exactly the opposite pattern in Germany, where financially successful component makers outspent their less successful counterparts. However, once again, despite the different approaches between the United States and Germany, successful companies in both countries spent about the same relative to sales.

✦ ✦ ✦

THE FINDINGS of our U.S. and German surveys support each other and reinforce a few basic beliefs about good management.

+ Achieving simplicity is a far more valuable contribution than delivering the capability to manage complexity. In both the United States and Germany, those managements that seek to simplify their problems before they develop sophisticated tools and systems to master complexity are more often rewarded with economic success.

+ Being market-driven rather than internally driven is a hallmark of success in both national environments. Market-driven managements are truly responsive to customers in every function of their business. In Germany, greater customer responsiveness results in faster product development times and lower selling, general, and administrative costs. In the United States, being market-driven means spending above-average amounts on sales, marketing, and new-product development costs. In both cases, successful companies buck accepted industry practice to deliver superior customer value.

+ Exposure to global competition, painful though it often is, helps create a healthy and competitive industry. The German machinery and component manufacturers have learned from competing with their European counterparts that simplicity is a key factor for success. They will soon learn that beyond simplicity lies productivity as the major test manufacturing companies must meet.

—A. Steven Walleck

INDEX

✦ ✦ ✦ ✦ ✦ ✦ ✦ ✦ ✦ ✦ ✦ ✦ ✦

short feedback loops in, 105, 106

Economies of scale, in-house and out-
    source, 61–62, 66, 72
Electronics industry, 79, 83, 92,
    94–95, 111
Employees
    compensation systems for,
        178–179, 197–198
    in maintaining manufacturer and
        supplier partnerships, 72–77
    motivating, 177–178
    in product development, 83–85,
        105, 107–108
    promoting high productivity levels
        in, 159–160, 161, 186,
        187, 197
    qualifications and flexibility of,
        27–28, 176–177
    training, 179–181, 203
Entrepreneurship
    in cost/benefit responsibility,
        167–168
    in delegation of responsibility,
        169–172
    in market and customer orienta-
        tion, 165–167
Equity, as performance indicator,
    4–6

Factor costs, 60–61, 66
Family of parts interfaces, 66
Flexible manufacturing systems
        (FMS)
    utilizing and operating, 149–150
    at Yamazaki, 25–26
Ford, 79
Freeze point, 13
    product variety and shifting,
        46–47, 48
Functional module interfaces, 65, 66
Functional organizational structure,
    165, 166

cost/benefit responsibility in,
    167–168
teams in, 185–186

German companies
•   compared with U.S. companies,
        187, 192–194
    in product development and
        design, 199–202
    in productivity, 196–198,
        199–200, 203–204
    in profitability, 194–199
    logistics in, 117, 118–119, 126,
        131–132
    organizational structure in, 27,
        157, 160, 163–165,
        166–167, 169, 170, 171,
        174–175, 176–177,
        178–179
    product development in, 81–83,
        86–87, 99, 101, 102, 105,
        107, 108, 110, 113
    technology in, 24, 134–135, 136,
        140, 148, 149, 151, 153
    vertical integration in, 54, 56, 60,
        63, 72–73
Greenfield locations, 123–125, 133

Hitachi, 112
Honda, 93, 110
    logistics of, 115–116
    sales, engineering, and develop-
        ment teams of, 103–104

IBM, 41, 104
In-house manufacturing
    marginal costs of, 59–60
    outsourcing costs versus, 60–64
    product development for, 97–101
    technological differentiation and,
        56, 58–59
    vertical integration for, 54, 77–78
Integrated product development

ABOUT THE AUTHORS

✦　✦　✦　✦　✦　✦　✦　✦

Felix Brück is a principal in the Munich office of McKinsey & Company. Felix joined McKinsey in Germany in 1983 and subsequently spent a year in Japan. He holds degrees in mechanical engineering from the University of Aachen and in business administration from the American Graduate School of International Management in Phoenix, Arizona. Before joining McKinsey he worked for three years in production engineering at Robert Bosch GmbH.

Mr. Brück is author of Chapters 2 and 5.

Raimund Diederichs is a principal in McKinsey's Vienna office. Raimund joined the firm in 1982. He holds a degree in mechanical engineering from the University of Aachen and an M.B.A. from INSEAD. Before joining McKinsey he worked for two years as a process engineer at Procter & Gamble, spending one year in the United States.

Mr. Diederichs is author of Chapter 4.

Rolf-Dieter Kempis is a principal in McKinsey's Düsseldorf office. Rolf-Dieter joined the firm in 1983. He holds degrees in mechanical engineering and economics from the University of Aachen. Before joining McKinsey he spent two years with Thyssen Steel AG, using operations research methods to develop an automated, EDP-compatible production management system.

Dr. Kempis is author of Chapter 1.

Jürgen Kluge is a principal in McKinsey's Düsseldorf office. Jürgen joined the firm in Düsseldorf in 1984 and spent some time working in the automotive industry in Brussels. He studied physics in Cologne and Essen, obtaining a Ph.D. in experimental physics, during which he developed high-frequency electronics for a U.S. laser company.

Dr. Kluge is author of Chapter 3.

Günter Rommel is managing director of McKinsey's Tokyo office. Günter joined the firm's German office in 1980 and subsequently spent a year and a half in Tokyo. He holds degrees from the Technical Universities of Stuttgart and Munich in electrical engineering, business administration, economics, and law and obtained his Ph.D. in investment planning.

Dr. Rommel is author of the Introduction and of Chapters 6 and 7.

A. Steven Walleck was, until his retirement at the end of 1993, a director in McKinsey's Cleveland office. Steve joined the firm in Düsseldorf in 1971 and moved to Cleveland in 1973. He holds a bachelor's degree in English literature and an M.B.A. from Harvard.

Mr. Walleck is author of the Postscript.

DATE DUE			
OCT 07 '96			
NOV 18 '96			
APR 1 4 1997			